CHANGES NATURE THROUGH THE SEASONS

JAMES M. TOTO

outskirts press

"Only after the last tree has been cut down. Only after the last river has been poisoned. Only after the last fish has been caught. Only then will you find that money cannot be eaten"

Cree Indian Proverb

Renewal

Ashen clouds obscure the light of day. A shadowy haze darkens a shrouded sky. The stems of dried out perennial flowers remain as reminders of what once was. Grassy meadows fade to brown. The nurturing sun has betrayed them to winter's frozen touch. The faded fields do not stand at death's door, yet . The high plant diversity in meadows more or less guarantees that there will also be a great diversity of animals. A variety of herbivores will be on hand to consume all the different plant species and they in turn will supply food for any number of carnivores from spiders to beetles, birds and foxes. Invertebrates such as butterflies, bees, and hoverflies will collect nectar from the flowers. Birds such as Goldfinches may visit to eat the seeds of thistles and composite plants. The leaves and stems of grasses and other plants provide food for caterpillars and other herbivorous animals. The dead tussocky bases of perennial grasses and the accumulation of leaf litter provide shelter and food for springtails, mites, and woodlice. Beneath this is the world of the soil, which is again seething with life. The soils of meadows contain high numbers of earthworms so moles will also be present, tunneling underground and feasting on the worms. The worms actually provide food for a surprising variety of mammals. Foxes will also eat worms, learning techniques from their elders to successfully extract them.

Small mammals such as field mice, voles, and shrews are common in meadows. Larger mammals such as white tailed deer will graze in meadows, particularly when the first spring flushes of grass start to grow. Perhaps the most conspicuous invertebrates of meadows are the butterflies. The caterpillars of all these butterflies feed on specific species of native wild grasses. Every leaf on every tree showed its real color. As days get shorter and nights become longer, trees prepare for winter and the next growing season by blocking off flow to and from a leaf's stem. This process stops green chlorophyll from being replenished and causes the leaf's green color to fade. Each weather-beaten giant will be renewed when the variable sun burns brightly again. Roots confined by snow and ice will be freed. Dense growth spreads beneath a distant tree line where every trunk darkened by melted snow stands in defiance of the north wind. Although still dormant, internal processes continue to occur within each tree throughout winter. Loosely analogous to hibernation in animals, trees undergo changes that allow them to survive the cold, dry conditions of winter. Like leaf –drop, acclimation is prompted by changes in the photoperiod. The sap of trees becomes rich in sugars. The sugar stops the sap from freezing. In other words, it acts as antifreeze. The deciduous trees lose their leaves in autumn but the branches already have buds which contain next year's leaves.

Just like seeds and roots, the buds of trees can "tell" when winter has passed and spring has arrived. Some trees only open their buds when there are a certain number of hours of daylight. Other trees need to pass through a cold period before the buds open. Most trees by the end of the growing season have formed terminal buds which remain through the winter and are destined to continue that growth the following spring. Flower buds are generally stouter than leaf buds. All trees produce flowers, but only a select few are showy enough to attract our attention. White, star-like blooms appear on service berry before the leaves of the tree unfold. Showy lavender eastern redbud trees are found along woodland borders. Flowering dogwood trees are found on wooded slopes. Their ornate blooms are actually composed of four large petal-like white bracts which surround a small yellow-green cluster composed of the true flowers. Very early, when the frost has barely left the ground in low moist areas, you may find the delicate, inconspicuous, star-shaped flowers of spicebush. Later, after the trees have begun to leaf out, look for the yellow and orange, cup-shaped flowers of the tulip poplar (you may have to look up very high). The flowers are a big draw for hummingbirds and honeybees. A mature tree can produce eight pounds of nectar, which bees are able to convert into four pounds of dark amber honey. Some tree blossoms are a challenge to see since they occur at the tops of trees or are very small.

But, they all add up to the necessary ingredients for a beautiful woodland in spring. Look at the woodlands with new eyes this spring, appreciating the native blooming plants. Enjoy the soft weather and long awaited flowering plants. Blooming woodland trees offer a perfect complement to sparkling springtime skies and the perfect antidote to winter. Each resilient hardwood prepares for the coming revival. On the ground, tender plants push forth from insulated confinement. Woody limbs eager to open their delicate new buds awaken. Each fragile new bud will burst open to reveal hidden leaves and flowers.

An intense flame will flare initiating fresh, new life. Fiery warmth will liquefy frozen water releasing its cool content for thirsty roots. Mild weather will encourage lush, green growth from seed to flower to seed again. All things alive will be set in motion. Compensation for surviving winter's wrath will come in the form of lovely colors and beautiful form. After a long, gray winter, the first blooms of spring are a welcome sight. At the end of winter, a scene of somber tones-black, grays and browns greets guests of the deciduous forest. Then, in brilliant contrast, the sun shines through the leafless canopy and falls upon a luminous array of small trees with blossoms so conspicuous they gladden the heart of those who long for spring. With the impending return of springtime comes a new found sense of newness and rebirth of everything all around us. There is truly something amazing about springtime.

It is difficult to fathom how a tiny seed, a corm, or a bulb can be placed in the soil, grow and bring forth a glorious array of blossoms. Often we find ourselves boasting about the beautiful flowers "we" have grown when they are in bloom in our garden. Yet, we must remember that we had very little to do with either their growth or their blooming. We only planted the seeds, fertilized and watered the soil; it was the hand of God that did the rest. Not only is Almighty God the Gardener, but the God who gives life to all things is also the Sun, the power that gives all that is alive the energy to grow and mature. Sometimes a garden is planted simply for its beauty. Flowers offer radiant artwork for the eyes and sweet perfume to any nose that draws near. Yes, the beauty alone is worth the work; however, most gardens are planted with the hope, desire, and even the need of producing some produce, some food. In nature, winter's freezing cold has a purifying effect that is necessary to keep pests and disease from completely overtaking plants. The trembling tree line gets a little relief from a shy sun peering from behind dark clouds. Spring brings squalls and then bouts of sun; switching back and forth as if Mother Nature can't decide on the day's weather pattern. Squalls can intersperse with sunny breaks and then at times you get everything in between. Unstable weather occurs more often in spring, when warm air begins to invade from lower latitudes, while cold air is still pushing from the Polar Regions. Winter still stubbornly defies.

The soil seal is still unbroken. Soon, however, it will be safe to emerge from hiding. For now, hope together with the anticipation of what will be serves as an incentive to wait until spring arrives. A slow-moving sun retreats behind dark clouds. The burning globe seems to have capitulated to its rival. A shadowy veil covers the sky. The sapphire brilliance of an unclouded sky has vanished ever since the dark curtain descended down upon the land. Grasses once green have turned to brown. Crystalline water falls in frozen flakes. Ice crystals dance upon the frigid wind. Fragile life lies idle beneath a veneer of white. The icy wind batters the trees. Dark silhouettes sway at the mercy of the relentless wind. Gray bark and silver tipped branches create a dismal combination of dull shades that make up the winter woodland tones. Everything all around appears pale and lifeless. Songbirds no longer sing to captivate secret admirers. For one, it burns calories. Second, it tempts predators. Those costs might be worth it if it meant attracting female attention, but that's not happening in winter. The male bird sings to declare his individual territory and to attract a mate. Mating is not one of the biological functions of the winter season, so songs are unsung until spring. Cheerful tunes sung by colorful migrants have been reduced to drab calls voiced by year round residents fluttering about under the cover of dense branches. During the long, silent interlude, idleness is interrupted by activity.

Great horned owls incubate white eggs, taking over the unused stick nest of a heron, or a hawk, often in the midst of winter storms. Cattails growing in roadside ditches may provide a perch for red-winged blackbirds. The bird's nasal call gives everyone a lift, for the red –wing is one of the earliest migrants to return each year, making it a convincing, reassuring sign of spring. Over the next couple of weeks or so, more males will trickle in to stake out their land claims. Then, in a few more weeks, there will be a huge incursion as the females return en masse from their wintering grounds down south, to select a mate and set up housekeeping. When the dark curtain lifts, a brightly shining sun will illuminate a renewed landscape. A brand new cast of characters will fill the stage. A deep blue sky will share its airy expanse with a softly glowing sphere. Together the two shall rule sovereign over the land of the living. When the clear, blue sky allows the shimmering sun to shine its brilliant light through its unclouded extent, the dismal clouds of winter will leave. The sun's luminosity will brighten the sky. Then, its sparkling light, reduced to memory, will become real again. All things alive will rejoice. Living things will express their appreciation through all the wonders of nature. Ice still forms on the hardened ground, but the soil warms a little more each day. Icicles drip from columns that will thaw completely in the bright sunshine. Only defiant areas that the sun's warmth cannot yet thaw out still defy the inevitable.

Soon the same water which froze the annuals and caused the perennials to retreat will liquefy and sustain dormant plants awakened from their sleep. In its frozen state, water affects fragile plant tissue. In its liquid state, water is crucial to all life. Plants need sunlight, nutrients from the soil, and water to live. Water is a major component of cells. It has a variety of properties not found in any other liquid. These properties are due to its molecular composition. The anticipated release of water back into the soil and changes in the weather do not deceive those that wait in the darkness below the surface of the soil. Patience is more than just a virtue. Something inside of us rejoices to see green foliage tips pressing upward through the soil, promising that warmer temperatures are just around the corner. At the same time, we experience a motherly anguish that nature will play a nasty trick and send a late winter freeze. March's lengthening days are not only a tonic for our winter blahs, but also a necessity for coaxing spring wildflowers into bloom. Unlike garden bulbs and domestic perennials that respond to warm temperatures and moisture, wildflowers take their cues to bloom directly from the sun. As daylight hours increase, so do the variety and numbers of blooms. Even though the temperature at the surface is variable, the temperature underground remains relatively constant. Resting perennials lie quietly within their insulated refuge. They seem to realize that it is not time to bore the cold earth.

Tranquil root stock is still reluctant to send out stems and leaves to explore the realm above ground. An internal timer prevents hasty emergence beyond the soil cover. Only when the duration of daylight increases, not the temperature, will new growth be initiated. Rock and soil encircle the somnolent like the walls around a castle of stone. Permission to leave underground concealment will be given. Roots will absorb water which once restrained them. New life will push up from within the soil cradle. Green growth will embrace the warm sunshine. The long winter spent in isolation will finally end. The cold, dark shroud will be lifted revealing an array of new sights and sounds to sleepy eyes. A joyous reunion will reunite those separated by the long winter. Fresh buds bloom, animals awaken and the earth seems to come to life again. Animals that spent the winter in hibernation come out of their dens. Those that traveled to warmer regions return. Many animals give birth in the spring. Winter coats are shed by those that donned them, and some animals may change coloration to blend in with their new surroundings. A celebration of life is approaching. The reawakening of springtime preludes the productivity of the growing season. Perennial flowers, flowering bulbs, trees, and shrubs that have been at rest during the cold months of winter are slowly coming back to life as is evident by tender new leaves and swollen buds. Spring is a busy time for trees.

Deciduous trees sprout leaves again, while Coniferous trees create new growth. The trees grow taller, sap flows, flowers bloom, and the trees begin to grow and reproduce. Maples have odd-looking flowers that lack true petals, but they will turn into the seed-bearing samaras, shaped like helicopter blades. Birches also have spring flowers, catkins, which resemble elaborate narrow cones. Oaks tend to leaf out between early and late spring. Male flowers, or catkins, look like long worms hanging from the oak tree in spring. Oak trees use the wind to pollinate the female flower. After pollination, the female oak flower starts to develop into an acorn. The American Beech flowers in the early spring just as its leaves are unfolding. The male flowers are small and yellow and clustered together into ball-like structures. The female flowers are even smaller and are found on the ends of new twig growth. Pollinated flowers form an edible nut which is eaten by many mammals and birds. Like many forest trees, hickory trees produce either male or female flowers and both types are found on the same tree. The male flowers are tiny and form an elongate drooping catkin, while the female ones are much less numerous, relatively large and eventually develop into hard-shelled nuts, surrounded by a woody husk. After a long, cold winter, one of the cheeriest sights a gardener can see is spring flowering bulbs coming up through the snow in the garden.

Spring flowering bulbs give a welcome splash of color to what is often an otherwise drab, muddy landscape in early spring. Delicate three-part flowers droop from thin, fragile stems of snowdrops. A sparkling gem has returned among the early spring flowering bulbs. These tough-as-nails little plants sprout even through snow - hence their name - and blossom while the calendar (and often the weatherman) says it's still winter. Each plant seems eager to show off its beauty. Tiny white flowers begin to bloom while snow still masks the half thawed ground—a delightful sight for the winter-weary. The snowdrop pops out in early spring, often pushing through the snow to appear. They can show up weeks before crocuses do and are among the earliest bloomers in the yard. Pure white petals delicately unfold in the warm sunshine. Waxy green tips previously hidden while the flowers were shut are now exposed. Greenish-gray, grass-like foliage adds the finishing touch to a living portrait. When the gently hanging spring pearls droop daintily, a new season has arrived. You can still feel the cold wind of winter, but spring is in the air. Snow drops are a sure sign that spring is on its way. The temperature gets warmer and the days longer and sunnier. And soon enough the other early spring flowers accompany the snow drops. Vivid colors brighten an otherwise drab landscape. Tiny, light sensitive petals open during the day and shut at night. Now is the time for bright spring color. Leaves are starting to appear on the trees. Flowers are in bloom all around.

Tired foliage continues to reap the benefits of the sun's awesome power even after colored petals become insignificant. Nutrients taken in will be stored in the bulb. When the last flower of spring fades away other flowers will dignify the summer scenery. When the last flower of summer dulls still others will complement the fall foliage. Meanwhile, the elegant spring blooming flowers stir up emotion at a time when there is often little to be emotional about. The luster of each colored petal represents the embodiment of love which all flowers have come to symbolize. The warmth of springtime ignites the inner warmth of the heart. Good bye, snow! Good bye, ice! Good bye, winter! Snow disappears from every crevice and frees up freshwater. Dormant trees begin to bud, leaves and flowers start to unfurl. Our excited spirits soar. Springtime at last! It may seem like it takes forever to get here, but faithfully she arrives nonetheless. The budding and blooming of the trees and the returning misty splashes of bright green on the branches all signal that spring is upon us. The arrival of spring is something that makes us rejoice. The vernal season is synonymous with flowers, sunlight, warmer temperatures and longer days. It is a time of flourishing and of expectation of the summer to come. The hardest days of winter are behind and we long to enjoy the colorful great outdoors. It is the perfect moment to gaze at the stars around a bonfire with friends. When spring arrives, with it comes much more than flowers.

An entire new set of constellations is painted in the night sky. The coming of spring ushers in improved seeing conditions, and along with it, a few seasonal constellations that had been out of view for some time. The night sky seen in springtime is especially majestic. Although northern hemisphere observers can see scores of constellations in the sky all year long, there are six major constellations generally identified with springtime. There are Ursa Major, Boötes, Leo, Cancer, Virgo and Hydra. With a shape that resembles a twisting snake, Hydra takes up slightly more than 3% of the night sky, making it the largest pattern of stars observed from Earth. Virgo is only slightly smaller than Hydra, and the largest zodiacal constellation. The Ursa Major constellation is famous for the Big Dipper asterism. Formed by the seven brightest stars found in the constellation, the Big Dipper is one of the most beloved and recognizable patterns of stars. Boötes is another of the six major spring constellations. Boötes is a very popular constellation because it contains the renowned Kite asterism, one of the most discernable shapes seen in the night sky. The Leo constellation is easy to find in springtime: just look for a group of stars shaped like a backwards question mark. This asterism is known as the Sickle, and it lies within the Leo constellation. Cancer is a spring constellation also included in the Zodiac, and it is found between Leo and Hydra.

And forever since then, Cancer and the other constellations have stayed above us in our night sky as a reminder of the remarkable feats we can accomplish if we set ourselves to them. Just start by looking at the stars and constellations and let yourself dream! The season between the lion and the lamb brings with it a song in every tree. As the season progresses it becomes a noisy but colorful affair. How can you tell it's springtime? Just open the window and listen to the enchanting trills of migrating songbirds. Brightly plumed songbirds begin arriving from far away wintering areas. Having spent the winter in warmer climes, these springtime crooners are returning to breed and raise their young. The first wave of migrating neotropics gets underway with the arrival of yellow-rumped warblers, blue-headed vireos, hermit thrushes, ruby-crowned kinglets, and chimney swifts. Another surge of spring migrants will appear in early May and then peak in late May, when the influx of songbirds will include American redstarts, ruby-throated hummingbirds, and several different warblers. Every year, at this time, wayward migrants, bound for other parts of the country, find their way here. This is an exciting time of the year for avian enthusiasts as fond feathered friends return to backyard feeders, forest and field. Many spring wildflowers begin to bloom as soon as the snow melts and temperatures begin to inch up. The flowers have to make a run for it before the leaves on the tall hardwood trees begin to block the sunlight.

A grand celebration of life is only just beginning. Mother Nature's jewels, clad in their finest attire, prepare for a spectacular renewal. Tiny, spring blooming flowers, just starting to poke their heat activated spears through the cool, moist soil, awaken from rest. Subtle hints of newly emerging flowers thrusting up through the soft soil lessen winter's melancholy. Although the show may be brief, it results in feelings of new hope. It's amazing how such small wonders can bring with them such great joy. The beauty that each elegant floral surprise brings to mind with each unfurling leaf and every unfolding flower sets in motion a joy that lasts through the seasons. The beauty is fleeting, however, and should be appreciated. They have a small window of sunshine between snowmelt and leaf-out in which to grow, flower, be pollinated, and produce seeds. By mid-June the deciduous trees that tower high above have cloaked the forest floor in deep shade. Spring ephemerals disappear in the heat of the summer, retreating underground until next year. An array of colors, shapes, and sizes refreshes the frayed landscape. The renewed scenery shines brilliantly with a glow of color. Every tender leaf and petal announces the arrival of a new season. The generosity that each tiny flower expresses is admirable. The disclosure of hidden secrets is short lived. Soon the early spring blooming wonders will move quietly back into concealment. It is a privilege to view the fleeting beauty of each bloom.

Enjoy the warmth of the empowered sun as the spring bulbs do for the seasons come to pass quickly. Lengthening days and warmer temperatures trigger responses in nature. Blooming, molting, migration, and breeding are cued to the length of days. The reason for the seasons is the celestial movement of the Earth as it orbits the sun. In summer, the Northern Hemisphere tilts toward the sun, and in winter it is the opposite. In spring and fall, the Earth's axis is tilted neither toward nor away from the sun. From late March through early June, the woodlands come alive with beautiful wildflowers. The first signs are the early spring flowers emerging out of the soggy ground. They need to grow, flower, and set seed quickly, because once the trees leaf out, the sunlight that powers all this activity will be obscured by the dense canopy, leaving these wildflowers in deep shade. Three- petaled trillium initiate the beginning of the festival of floral color in the fertile woods. Harbinger-of-spring only grows about three inches high and are frequently over looked during woodland walks. The showy three-part flowers of hepatica bloom on a slender stalk. By April, the woodland floor is alive with dozens of wildflower species. Trout lilies, named for their speckled leaves that resemble a trout's scales, bloom yellow and white. Virginia bluebells, with their trumpet-like flowers, are among the most-common and most attractive wildflowers. Clusters of toothwort gather under tall oak trees.

While purplish-blue is the common color of wild violets, they are also found in yellow and white. A treasure trove of enchanting springtime flowers set a wonderful contrast against the typical greens and browns of a woods. To see these spring beauties is a real joy, so leave them in the ground for everyone to enjoy. Always leave no trace and never disturb any wildlife or pick any wildflowers. It's best to take nothing but memories and leave nothing but footprints. Once the weather warms a little more in April and May the forest floors are carpeted with many different kinds of flowers of all colors. This beautiful bloom of color is quite a spectacle. It's a very nice change from the grip of winter that hangs on for several months. Trees too come alive in springtime. Tree buds are tiny sculptures, joys of winter and early spring that are too often left unappreciated. The spice bush and serviceberry are in bloom, blending a palate of tiny yellow flowers with bright white ones. Leaf buds are bursting green. The swollen red buds of silver maple are ready to bloom. The very first tree to bloom in the spring is the silver maple. It can beat the crocus and is a major boon to early -waking pollen and nectar eaters. Honey bees and bumble bees are already out and about. All the pollinators are busy already. If your nose is sneezy and running, eyes are watering, and your head hurts, it's no surprise. The arrival of spring has produced blooms all over the place and the pollen that comes with it.

The smooth outer covering that encircles the uppermost branches resembles the covering that once protected the trunk of the tree when it wore a younger bark veneer. The bark of the older trees peels away readily. Older trees also develop a flared basal trunk that merges with its large surface roots. Silvery terminal branches reach skyward so that the leaves that are unfolding can better capture the sun's energy. Branching spreads outward from a pedestal of solid wood forming a broad, oval arch. Red tipped twigs contain small bundles of growing tissue that will grow into either a branch, a leaf, or a flower. Flowers of silver maple emerge long before the leaves and give a reddish cast to the otherwise bare twigs as early as late winter, and last into early spring. Beyond the reddish treetops a blue-gray sky looms. A gentle breeze sways the large hardwoods back and forth. The outline of their bare branches moves gently in the wind. Wild birds will begin to build nests in preparation for egg laying. Either concealed on the ground, or suspended in a low bush, a well-made cup of grass and leaves may contain pale green, brown-spotted eggs belonging to a song sparrow. An over wintering eastern bluebird inspects a tree cavity, enlarged by a woodpecker, for use as this season's nesting chamber. Mourning doves lay the first of several clutches of eggs on a loosely made nest of twigs. Male goldfinches turn gold. Each morning the sound of singing birds rings in the early part of the day.

Affection in the form of a song permeates the silence of a new day. Few things are as interesting, lively, and beautiful as birds. They

While purplish-blue is the common color of wild violets,
they are also found in yellow and white.

brighten up the dark days of winter and fill our woodlands and gardens with their music. Chickadees will whistle "Phoebe", nuthatches will honk like a tiny horn, titmice will screech "Peter, Peter, Peter", and woodpeckers will hammer out their heart's desire with their beaks against hollow branches. These are all winter-resident birds. They're here all winter because they know how to do it. The trees are filled with songbirds, their little chests puffed out with springtime passion. What they are singing about is anyone's guess.Perhaps they sing a heartfelt love song to their mates sitting on a nest and incubating a clutch of eggs. Or perhaps they sing more of an uninteresting song telling others that "This is my tree…" Bird song can be a natural marvel of intense beauty. But our enjoyment is incidental to the main purpose, which is one bird communicating with others. Birds became the world's master musicians in order to convey to potential mates, rivals and predators all the important things they have to say, from " Go away !" to " Come on!" The musical detail would have impressed the greatest composers. Song allows the bird to "speak". It is the perfect medium for communicating over long distances, or when it is hard to see the singer - and the audience. For example at night or in dense vegetation. Sound travels in all directions; it can penetrate through or around objects.

Birds sing to communicate, and you can blame that initial morning song on the males, who sing to announce that they are alive, alert and ready to defend their territory. Early blooming perennials show off their colors too. After the sun settles, the colored petals follow its retreat. Their blooms close as sunlight fades. They reopen their flowers when the sun reappears. For the tiny, spring flowering bulbs, the time for sharing colors is nearing its end. As the spring blooming bulbs reach the stunning peak of their visual extravaganza they deserve a well-earned round of applause for their performance. Spring, for the most part, is the time for perennials to take their place in the landscape. Perennial flowers put on the stage in the fading footsteps of the retreating early spring flowering bulbs. The perennial flowers have been resting as roots and rhizomes waiting for the chance to venture above the soil surface again. Newly emerging flowers bid a fond farewell to their departing companions. Reliable friends re-united after a long separation epitomize the essence of springtime. A few perennials mingle among the tulips by late spring as others are beginning to grow. Spring-and summer-blooming flowers, each with its own distinctive shape, color and size create a showy landscape presence. Vibrant color attracts insects and birds to the painted al-lurement. Bell-shaped flowers grace gardens with fairy tale charm.

They may be tiny blossoms, peeping shyly from beneath pro-tective foliage, or large, bold clusters of blooms cascading from the branches of stately trees. Clusters of white bell-shaped flowers droop from stems under their own weight. Bells from humble to haughty adorn bulbs, shrubs, and perennials of all types. Their seductive scent attracts some of the first insects to come out. The newly emerged in-sects take advantage of a fresh supply of pollen and nectar. The sounds of woodland birds adds to the ambience of the woods in springtime. Deer seek shelter in the woods during the day, often concealing a new born fawn amongst the wildflower growth. Bees collect prized pol-len from ample anthers. Their benefit as pollinators goes beyond the fear of being stung. Butterflies visit abundant nectaries. Their colorful cloaks shimmer in the bright sunlight. Elegant patterns combine with captivating color rivaling the most colorful flowering plant. Blissful songs sung by transient songbirds echo from the adorned branch-es of woodland trees. The bubbling call of a house wren signals an announcement to other birds. Colorful singers take a much needed break from their long, physically demanding journey. The leafed out

A treasure trove of enchanting springtime
flowers set a wonderful contrast against the
typical greens and browns of a woods.

trees will soon support nests. Small woody trees adorned with flowers beautify the woods. Redbud trees come into full bloom. Extremely showy trees whether in flower, in fruit, or in autumn coloration, flowering dogwood trees compliment the lower layer of the woods.

Wildflowers such as trout lily and bloodroot thrive there in April. Tender leaflets unfurl in the warmth of a brand new day. You may hear the howling of foxes and the croaking of frogs resulting in temporary vernal pools being swollen with frog spawn and foxes accompanied by pups. Winter den sites will be cleared out. Ground dens dug next to discarded logs or in thick brier and vine growth will be vacated to reap the bounty of a season of abundance. Red fox kits play aboveground near the earthen mound of their maternity dens. Excavated earth, cache mounds, holes where food has been retrieved, and scraps of discarded bones and feathers indicate the presence of a den site. Young ones will acquire the habits of their teachers. Spring weather is unpredictable. Sometimes there is cold rain, and at other times high heat. Rain is almost a daily occurrence in spring. With that rain comes amphibians. Frogs breed in vernal pools. Turtles are starting to emerge from brumation, after a long winter's rest. Spring peeper males gather in small pools of water and sing choruses to attract females. Woodchucks begin awakening from hibernation in late February or early March. Overwintering insects such as lady bird beetles have been sheltering in the soil, under leaves, rocks, or logs, or inside the stalks of dried perennials. American woodcock males perform their famous sky dance. Ruby -throated hummingbirds gather soft dandelion down, strong and stretchy spider silk, and bits of leaves and lichen for their nests.

They are so tiny, yet so perfect. Monarch butterflies begin their incredible migration from Mexico. Animals that hibernated over winter appear on the first warm days. A rebirth will occur. All will rejoice in the warmth of springtime. The life-giving soil will nurture autumn's seeds. Tender leaflets will unfurl in the warmth of a new day. Tightly closed buds will open exposing colorful flowers. New shoots will reach for the bright glow of the fiery sphere. Spring brings the promise of renewal. Winter's piercing reflection is given life in springtime. The forest supports a wondrous array of flora and fauna. Trees breathe life into our lungs. Dogwood trees bloom among leaves of green. Lilac blooms contribute to the unforgettable smell of a gentle spring breeze. Serviceberry shrubs are early bloomers in April. Nature's palette holds the colors of a remarkable abundance of wildflowers during April and May. A grand culmination of colorful spring blooming flowers occurs in May. White mayflower, trillium, and toothwort awaken from their silent repose. Yellow marsh marigold, buttercup, and the familiar dandelion beautify a bright new world. Pink wild geranium and lovely lady's slipper brighten the greenery. Red wake robin and fire pink lend a splash of color to the woodland tones in springtime. Wild blue phlox, bluebell, and tiny speedwell decorate the ground they share with the trees.

Spring is a season of natural drama: awakenings, departures and arrivals, territorial disputes, courtship songs and displays, nest building, egg laying, and frenzied food gathering. By mid spring, the winds and rains have calmed. There is a new calmness in the air. All of nature is in meaningful motion. Tender buds on trees have unfolded. Flowers are abundant and fragrant. Everything is that particular shade of green that we see only once a year. The vernal new borns, having outgrown natal teeth, feathers, and pelts are now loaded with hormones. All-too ready to venture out on their own. Spring is a time when everything is growing and bursting into life. Birds are singing, leaves are unfolding, butterflies are starting to be seen and mammals are beginning to wake from their winter sleep. The doldrums of winter fade to the wealth of spring. As winter finally fades away, all things gear up for the warmer months ahead. Natural wonders can be viewed in every season, but a sunny day in springtime is difficult to match at any time.

Spring is a glorious time of year in the woodlands with green buds and blossoms filling the trees and wildflowers quietly emerging from their winter slumber.The woods come alive with color, casting hues of white,blue,purple, and yellow. These dainty plants grow in beds of moss and leaf litter where larger plants will not easily crowd them. Immerse yourself in early morning bird choruses as you walk the woodland path. They start very early, before dawn, and continue until the morning wanes toward midday. Their melodic calls inter- weave with the sunlight to brighten the new day. One of the many good things about spring is that without it, and without the absence imposed by fall and winter, we flawed mortals might fail to appreci- ate the beauty around us.Would the new leaves and flowers be so wonderful to our small minds if they hadn't been absent?A walk in the woods during springtime is always a delight.

The coming of spring is considered a rebirth. Fresh buds open, animals awaken and the earth seems to come to life again. Birds be- gin nesting and migratory species begin the long flight from winter to summer homes. Hibernating animals leave their dens and burrows. Spring is a time of renewal of nature, every day more and more flow- ers are in bloom and fresh,green leaves appear on trees. The seeds planted last autumn that have germinated over the winter have be- come new seedlings beginning to break through the frozen earth, and signs of renewal and hope begin to stir within us. The air seems fresher, the step lighter and spring fever fills the heart.

Colors

Step carefully when walking within the forest in spring. The woods are alive! The treed passage from the forest edge into the deep woods feels like a comforting embrace. A sudden trill overhead or a rustle in the underbrush signals the exciting prospect of a wildlife encounter. A relaxing walk offers a fresh prospective each season, from the pastel bed of delicate spring wildflowers and summer's cool canopy of refreshing green, to autumn's curtain of blazing reds and luminous yellows. Spring brings one of the most dazzling wildflower displays seen anywhere in the world. But, the display is short-lived. Soon, tree buds break and the burst of leaf growth begins to cast a veil of shade on the forest floor. Spring wildflowers bloom abundantly. They must produce flowers attractive to pollinators so that seeds may be formed in hast before the light stealing leaves of the forest trees completely unfold capturing the sun's powerful emission. Soft sunlight nurtures them in their soil confinement. A mosaic pattern of color complements the huge trees surrounding them. Festive Virginia bluebells chime with each breath of air as if ringing in a new season. Trillium show off their solitary white flowers. They grow in scattered groups that seem to cover an endless tract. Trout lilies poke up through the leaf litter to investigate the woodland realm. Tiny rue anemones display an umbel of white.

And everyone knows that "Jack" is always there in mid to late spring, preaching to the rest of the forest from his pulpit. Cautiously peering up through the leaf covered forest floor the woodland wildflowers explore a new world. The beauty of springtime is wonderful to watch. The splendor, however, is fleeting for quickly conditions will change. New buds will open revealing leaves. Energy storing leaves lean toward the penetrating light. The unobstructed path taken by bright sunbeams to the base of the leaf strewn forest floor will be blocked by greenery. As the length of days get shorter in autumn and temperatures decrease, trees set themselves in a dormant state, only to burst into life in spring. The result will be unbearable for the living treasures that grow in the rich organic soil. Competition for sunlight will be too difficult for them. Blooms will fade. Leaves will wither. For everything there is a time. The time for woodland color has come and gone. Retreat below ground is inevitable. Many woodland wildflowers are ephemeral; they go dormant soon after blooming, as soon as their seed is ripe. This strategy evolved because when the woods become shaded and dry in summer, foliage becomes a liability for small, delicate woodland wildflowers. Ephemeral wildflowers, such as trillium, bloodroot, and wild geranium spread out wide green foliage to absorb summer's dim light, instead of going dormant. The final hour has come for the woodland beauties. Dense shade does not allow lots of blooming.

The woodland wildflowers bloom before the leaves of the trees develop. They are the leaders in a race against the trees to bloom, become pollinated, and make seeds before the tree leaves block the sunlight. Each year, the eastern deciduous forest puts on a generous display of wildflowers. Native woodland wildflowers have evolved

And everyone knows that "Jack" is always there in mid to late spring, preaching to the rest of the forest from his pulpit.

a life cycle that coincides with available sunlight. Rapid growth and flowering occurs from late March thru May, then tree leaves develop and significantly reduce sunlight available to plants on the forest floor. As tree leaves develop, wildflower growth and development is greatly reduced. Some early spring woodland wildflowers such as May apple become dormant by midsummer and will not reappear until the following spring. Shade-loving summer and fall -blooming wildflowers occur along forest edges or in dappled shade, even they will not grow in dense shade. Shade-loving wildflowers have several basic needs: light shade, adequate moisture, soils high in organic matter, and a leaf mulch that persists throughout the year. Most woodland wildflowers prefer an acidic soil that is rich in humus. You may still find a few Dutchman's breeches in bloom. The lacy blue- green leaves of Dutchman's breeches look like their relative bleeding heart. Bloodroot leaves are visible, but the flowers have long since shown their glory. Woodland wildflowers naturally grow in areas where leaves and other plant debris accumulates and becomes part of the soil environment.

Organic matter and mulch is critical for their growth; it helps hold moisture, keeps the soil cool and helps the soil stay loose and well aerated. The toad is a denizen of the forest floor, where it feeds on the many invertebrates which themselves feed on the decaying leaves that abound there. Among the most terrestrial of amphibians, toads have a thin skin and depend on the high humidity (80-90%) of the forest floor to survive. Box turtles also thrive here. Like the toads, they also feed on the invertebrates of the forest floor. Jefferson salamanders, awakened by the warm rains of spring, navigate from natal pools to introduce themselves to others, where they will mate and deposit eggs. Gentle spring rains, runoff or rising ground water assist in filling vernal pools providing essential breeding habitats for amphibians and insects, who lay their eggs and spend the early part of their lives there. Although these depressions may not look like important habitats, they are vital to many species of salamander, frog and insect that get a relatively predator-free start in life there. Vernal pools may look like lifeless spring puddles, but they are important amphibian habitats. They dry up during the summer, usually. But when they're full they're full of life. They are as welcome and fleeting as the first spring wildflowers peeking up through last year's leaves. The gelatinous eggs of red spotted newts will hatch into aquatic larvae,which will live in the vernal pools for about three months then they shed their gills and move onto land to live as efts for 3-4 years before returning to the water at maturity.

Tiny piping tree frogs will begin their annual ritual of song announcing the arrival of spring in the woods near the small seasonal depressional wetlands. Normally very seldom seen, spring peepers become more noticeable during their breeding season. Males get to the breeding ponds first, and will be calling when the females arrive. The high pitched "peep, peep" call is a classic announcement call. When the amphibian serenade closes the day, we know that spring has come to the wet woods. Wildflowers bloom in brilliant circles of color that follow the receding shoreline of the pools. New flowers replace those that have bloomed and regressed. The colorful spring blooming flowers will return. The splendor of the spring blooming wildflowers will remain in our hearts long after their beauty disappears from our eyes. The only constant thing about the seasons is that they always come and go. The promise of the growing season reminds us of the prosperity of summer. Summer brings flowers, and permits us to admire nature's work. Who can argue that nature paints some of the most beautiful pictures ever viewed by human eyes? Native wildflowers portray a palate of rich and vibrant colors that inspire feelings of awe and tranquility. The potentials of summer will soon replace the excitement of spring. Summer is the season of plenty. This is the time when trees bear fruit, the time when the forest fills up with undergrowth and new life. The reality of fall and scarcity of winter is forgotten as the woody shrubs bear fruit and new growth. Summer gives rise to events that bring to culmination all which has occurred since the withered stalks of autumn fell to winter's reaping sickle. Flowering plants grow in the warmth of a new season of hope. Resting perennials awaken from slumber. Restless roots search for nourishment. Freed from icy impoundment, delicate root hairs begin spreading out away from the deep penetrating tap root. Fragile roots absorb vital nourishment from the thawed soil, drawing up nutrients from the water that once held them captive. A bright sun has aligned itself beyond the furthest extent of a clear sky, shining down more directly on the land over which it rules by day. All the forest trees are now in full leaf. The powerful energy of the sun is caught by each light receptive leaf. Sturdy stems of perennials grow upward supporting delicate buds, which will open as flowers. Each bloom will open in a show of gratitude for having been given the opportunity to express itself. Summer flowers add bright color and beauty to the landscape through the heat of summer until frost. Flowers and seasons are intimately bound to each other. Spring arrives at different times depending on where you live, but the sequence of blooms is similar in most places. The charm of summer's painted petals serves a purpose beyond visual appeal. Each beautiful bloom is a receptacle for reproduction. Brightly pigmented petals surround the reproductive parts of the flowering plant.

The gentle glow of color and the sweet fragrance of each petaled jewel attracts pollinators that may, in the process of gathering pollen and nectar for their own needs, stimulate stamens and pollinate pistils. Summer is a time of frantic activity for animals busy rearing young and finding food. Finding nest sites and areas of shade become important and adequate water supplies are vital. Adults must find food both for their growing young and to build up their own body stores to help them survive the winter months. In the woods, white tail fawns are born. Although it may seem to be a laid back and lazy time for whitetail deer does, she's working to teach her fawns about life and working to get them off on their own. Look for large tracks together with smaller tracks in the soft mud. Red admiral butterflies search for nettles to lay their eggs upon. Although beautiful with wide-open wings, its blue, pink, and brown marbled underside is equally attractive. Colorfully clad fragile flyers visit the garden in the woods. There they share in the bounty of the fertile forest, renewed by the continuous addition of the remains of plants and animals, which once required the same nutrients that they now leave behind, for their own metabolic and physiological requirements. Summer is a season of abundance, producing a bounty of food in the form of both plants and animals. It's also a season of lots of duties for animal parents busy building and guarding nests and feeding, protecting, teaching, and caring for their young.

This is when insect life is most abundant. Honeybees move from flower to flower.

Pollination is a fortunate side effect: what the bees are after is sweet nectar, which they concentrate and convert to honey. Fireflies produce light via a chemical reaction. Few things typify warm summer evenings more perfectly than watching them blink on and off in the distance. The start of spring can be an unpredictable affair, but, is one of the best times to see insects. Spring is a really important time for bugs. Damp earth is the flower garden's canvas. The warmth of spring invites the seed to sprout. The summer sun nurtures the seed. Emerald leaves open. Color compliments seductive fragrance. Bright, warm colors bring serenity to the mind and fulfillment to the soul. A soothing smell never goes unnoticed or unappreciated. The beauty alone is reason enough to rejoice in viewing the annual display. Summer allows us to think about the unique beauty of each bloom. The summer rite represents the culmination of growth. The canna lily spends the summer producing large, tropical-looking leaves and then decides to bloom later. Coreopsis take awhile to get going in spring,but make up for it later. Long-lasting daisy-like flowers atop purple coneflower appear in an unusual shade of mauve-purple surrounding an iridescent red-orange , coned center. It's large ,showy purple flowers are part of a three-month long "coneflower extravaganza" from mid-June through September. Black-eyed Susan shows up in many gardens, and for good reason.

It tolerates poor soil and drought, and it blooms like crazy from summer to fall.

Always fresh, and always eye-catching, Shasta daisies start blooming in early summer and just don't stop, especially if the old flowers are removed regularly. It is a good-looking plant with large white daisy flowers that appear late spring through autumn. Dahlias come in just about every color, and late summer is their time to shine. With an array of different colors, shapes and sizes, dahlias bring life and beauty back to the landscape in late summer and into the fall months. Enjoy the summer flowers while they are in bloom for they are quickly gone. Fertilized flowers produce seeds. A destiny fulfilled, perennials return underground from which they arose, where they pass the winter. The colors of summer bring out emotions. Their beauty brings joy into the lives of people. Vivid shades lift the heart. Most early summer wildflowers are found along roadsides, in fields, or in lawns. But there are still a few wildflowers that can be found in the forest during

The late summer flowers thrive in the open fields,
in contrast to the grasses accompanying them.

late May and early June. Wildflowers adorn the woods in a rainbow of color. In purples, reds, blues and yellows these wildflowers are true natural wonders. All plants live or die with the weather. Hot weather coupled with generally dry soil causes plant stresses that range from sunburn to wilt to poor flower and fruit production. The harshness of a dry growing season plagued by inadequate rainfall can cause shallowly rooted annual flowers to die back or even die completely.

The fine roots, those that absorb water and nutrients, might die.

Annuals complete their life cycle within the space of one year. In other words, you plant a seed, it grows foliage, it flowers, seeds and then the plant dies, all in the same year. The whole objective of an annual is to produce seed and propagate. Pansies will fade as summer heats up. Verbenas have a delicate, airy appearance; they make good garden borders, coming into flower after the first riot of spring bloom has passed, and carrying gallantly on through the heat of midsummer when many of the perennials are quiescent. Low-growing phlox displays showy flowers that bloom in a multitude of shades filling the garden with color from spring through late summer. Strolling through the garden on a balmy summer day inhaling the sweet perfume of phlox you may become as captivated by phlox as the butterflies, bumble bees, and moths that pollinate it. Butterflies, bumble bees and an occasional hummingbird may find phlox irresistible, but its charms aren't restricted to these daytime pollinators. On summer evenings, as the sweet scent of phlox drifts across the garden, moths may be drawn to its flowers. Solitary daisy-like flower heads beautify the long stems of zinnia. Zinnias won't even get moving until the nights stay warm. While gardening is generally an avocation requiring patience, this isn't the case with zinnias, one of the quickest flowers to bloom from seed.

Long flowering petunias can be found in just about every color of the rainbow in solids, contrasting veins or edges, and star patterns. Petunias grow easily and add an elegant touch to the garden. As spring turns into summer, the cool day glow colors of vinca complement glossy green oval leaves. Whether the summer is dry or wet, hot or cold, annual vinca plugs along unfazed. As spring wears off and summer heat picks up, flowering plants –both annuals and perennials—bloom profusely. Most flowering annuals are fairly heat tolerant and can usually be revived with a few sips of liquid fertilizer. For some plants, stress from summer heat turns off the initiation of flowers. Plants that might otherwise direct their energy toward flower production must now divert their resources toward basic metabolic activity. Some plants might appear wilted during the hottest part of the day, but may unfurl their tired leaves after the blazing sun draws back. Delicate adornments curl up to conserve moisture and reduce evaporation. Internal processes occur at the cellular level in response to light intensity that permit, or prevent the absorption of water into and out of plant tissue via specialized structures. Survival during the heat of summer is insured by tiny epidermal structures, which serve as the frontier between the semi aquatic inner world of the leaf and the comparatively dry terrestrial environment outside. Safeguards regarded as necessary through evolutionary trial and error do not guarantee survival, especially when other environmental factors exist.

But heat nearly always has partners in crime. Moisture, wind, cloud cover and plant species can be just as important. Like heat, all four can affect how well plants' cooling system works. A plant can't cool itself without adequate soil moisture. At the same time, over watering can shut down plants' cooling system as fast as drought can. Not enough and too much are both bad. When seasonal temperatures rise rain totals tend to drop significantly. Add to that, the heat resistance of the plant itself, the humid summer winds, drying things out and reducing cloud cover and you get a four-part whammy that great-ly reduces plants' ability to tolerate the high temperatures. The main way plants cope with heat is a process called transpiration. Roots absorb water from the soil and send it up through the plant. Some of that water then evaporates from the leaves through tiny pores, called stomata. The evaporating water cools each leaf much like evaporat-ing sweat cools skin. But air that is not fully saturated with water vapor will dry the surfaces of cells with which it comes in contact. This transpired water must be replaced by the transport of more wa-ter from the soil to the leaves. Dry soil reduces water availability. It also signals the leaves' stomata to close. Wind shakes branches and leaves, causing stomata to close. Wind blows away the thin layer of cool air around each leaf and often scatters cloud cover.

Intense sunlight plays a role in stomata closure and rises leaves' internal temperature above the surrounding air temperature. Each of these factors contributes to the complete breakdown of leaf cells, which results in "heat scorch", it's a lot more than just that. Excessive heat makes things worse by disrupting the normal functions of in-ternal plant cells. One of the first processes affected is photosynthe-sis- the way a plant makes food. Many plants can recover from this disruption overnight, but only if nighttime temperatures cool off. If they don't, plants have cumulative effects-carryover stress from one day to the next. Fertile soil may turn to dust under the burning sphere. Under such drought conditions it becomes exceedingly more difficult to obtain the essential macronutrients and the lesser used micronu-trients, which are both normally mixed in among the collection of microorganisms residing in the soil; all indispensable to day to day maintenance of living plants. Compacted soil may no longer be able to absorb water and minerals, both much needed now more than before. Plants are 70-90% water, which is required for plant growth, manufacture of food, and nutrient transport. Because of water, plants experience feast or famine, flood or drought, air or suffocation. Plants get most of their water directly from soil surrounding their roots. Both water and air exists in the pore space surrounding individual soil particles and aggregates.

Ideally, about half the volume of soil surrounding roots should be solid mineral or organic material and about half pore space. In an ideal situation, about half the pore space should hold air and about half, water. Under such conditions, plant roots can get both the air and water they need. When soil is dry (most of its pores filled with air) roots cannot get enough water. Water is the stuff of life. Besides the direct effects of dry soil, a plant under stress becomes more susceptible to insect and disease problems that can attack a weakened plant. When soil is waterlogged (most of its pores filled with water) roots cannot get enough air. When environmental stresses strain available resources, the door that holds back insect pests and diseases opens. Insects seek out and cause problems for plants weakened by damage caused by environmental stress. Physically damaged plants present less of a challenge to ruinous bane. A plant weakened by environmental stress and damaged by insects is less likely to fully repair the damage done than would an unimpaired plant. Insects can be the cause of two types of damage to growing plants. The first is direct injury done to the plant by the feeding insect, which eats leaves or burrows into stems, fruit, or roots. The second type is indirect damage in which the insect itself seemingly does little or no harm but transmits bacterial, viral, or fungal infection to the plant. Insects are the most diverse species of animal living on earth.

Insects are the most adaptable form of life as their total numbers exceed that of any other animal group. The majority of insects are important to the environment.

For example, several insect species are predators or parasitoids of harmful pests. Others are pollinators, decomposers of organic matter, or produce valuable products such as honey or silk. Less than 0.5 percentage of the total number of the known insect species are considered pests. Depending on the point of view, insect pests can be defined as any insect in the wrong place. Insects spread disease from plant to plant. Plants infected with disease often spread their contagious ailment to nearby healthy plants which themselves are much more susceptible when carrying the added burden of high heat related stress. A garden is actually a natural micro-system at work. If you notice that plants have ragged, chewed or missing leaves, or holes in stems or branches, insects are the likely culprits. Insects can move into your garden and rapidly increase in numbers. The best thing you can do is to maintain a healthy garden. The first step to a healthy garden is a healthy soil. A healthy, biologically active soil will help keep the population of insects and the incidence of disease at tolerable levels. Healthy plants need healthy and happy living soil. Ample water and nutrients produce healthy plants that are much more resistant to pest damage. Plants need large quantities of water. Water typically makes up 80-95 % of the mass of growing plant tissue.

Plants have cell walls that allow the build up of turgor pressure within each cell.

Turgor pressure contributes to the rigidity and mechanical stability of non-woody plant tissue and is essential for many physiological processes including cell enlargement (plant growth), gas exchange in the leaves, transport of water and sugars, and many other processes. Without enough water in the cells, plants droop, so water helps a plant to stand up. Water carries dissolved sugar and other nutrients through the plant. So without the proper balance of water, the plant not only is malnourished, but it is also physically weak and cannot support its own weight. Only rain can offer relief. Heavy clouds darken the sky. Clouds are made up of water droplets. The water vapor in clouds condenses and forms what will become raindrops. The dark clouds, dense with water, will open releasing much needed rain down upon a parched land. Drifting high in the airy expanse, puffy white clouds are the most obvious feature of the sky. Remember when you were a kid and would look up at the skies to watch the clouds go by? Gazing up, you might see a few fluffy bunnies drift by, followed by a fleet of racing sailboats. Spiritually, emotionally and just plain visually they are better than any works of art. Clouds play an important role in the energy balance of earth. They cool the earth by reflecting sunlight back out into space. More importantly, clouds replenish our water supply. It's a never ending cycle but one that keeps the earth balanced.

The humid conditions of summer are favorable for the development of thunderstorms. Nutrients will be distributed with each coveted rain drop. Minerals previously locked up in the soil will be released. It would be heartbreaking if after waiting for winter to pass, and experiencing the fleeting beauty of spring, the sun warmed flowers of summer were reduced back to that from which they originated because of not enough rainfall. Summer's floral bouquet require lots of water to grow and do well. All plants require nutrients for growth. The annuals must produce flowers before their short life is completed. The seeds of today become the plants of tomorrow. The perennials must build up their roots so that they can exist as root stock after they retreat as winter's advance approaches. During the summer, the bright sun caresses each green leaf and every colored petal with its warm touch. During dry periods, it can appear as though the sun has betrayed the plants, which depend on its generosity. The summer sun makes a lot of heat and puts a lot of strain on plants. The midday sun is intense, especially during the summer, and the high temperatures that direct sunlight brings can burn plants quickly, especially the more sensitive types. Intense temperatures cause plants to wilt just when they should be starting their summer growth spurt. Most healthy plants can withstand periodic dryness without losing vigor.

However, shallow surface roots cannot withstand the stress of extreme heat which dries and cakes the soil in the top few inches. Some plants stop flowering and setting fruit when temperatures soar. Green plants love full sun on a warm day, but in high summer heat the sun can dry out plants and stop production. Plants will naturally stop setting fruit when daytime temperatures climb above 92 degrees Fahrenheit. Blooming on plants will stop, and fruits or blossoms will prematurely drop off the plant. After the green boon of spring, summer can seem harsh. The extreme heat and frequent dryness can be detrimental to plants. Extended periods of heat, which are common throughout July and August for most of the United States, can cause heat stress for trees and other plants. Plants, of course, rely on water to function normally. To keep cool, water travels through the plants' roots up to the leaves. It is then released through the underside of the leaves. When it is very hot, this process is accelerated, so plants run through their water fast. If transpiration is interrupted by stomatal closure due to water stress, a major cooling mechanism is lost. When stomata are open, transpiration increases; when they are closed, transpiration decreases. Even as flowers wilt in the heat of an unforgiving sun, activity continues in anticipation of the season to come. With the dog days of summer bearing down on us, some begin to long for a crisp fall breeze.

In the weedy grasslands, goldfinches gather thistle fluff to line a well-made cup of grass generally placed in a small shrub which will be filled first with eggs then with nestlings. Nesting coincides with the availability of weed seeds since their main source of food is seeds.

Flocks of cedar waxwings congregate on wild black cherry trees to pluck off ripe fruit only to vanish afterward. Waxwings also tend to nest late since gaping mouths are fed mainly on small fruits. Large gatherings of Canada geese enjoy what is left behind in harvested fields. There are always a few heads up, keeping watch. Duckweed covered sloughs provide wood duck and their broods shallowly flooded habitat with good vegetative cover that the ducks can hide and forage in. Migrating blue-winged teal rest in the wetlands en route to a southerly destination. Soon a grand exodus will begin. Fall migration of songbirds will get underway. Flocks of purple martins and barn swallows will assemble near the large ponds before fall migration. Soon you will see large flocks of blackbirds rolling amongst the clouds, or hear geese honking in flight after raising their young. You can be sure that there will be songbirds in the woodlands, shorebirds in the marshes, waterfowl on the wing, and hawks and eagles flying overhead on their way to their wintering grounds. It's the end of July and August looms. It's the time of year when summer is almost over. Before too long the leaves will begin to change colors. In the lives of many migratory birds, August marks the beginning of autumn. First year shorebirds have already departed their Arctic nesting grounds and have started to arrive in Northeast Ohio, where they will rest and feed before continuing on their long aerial journey to the Southern Hemisphere. Soon thereafter, Baltimore orioles and yellow warblers will be the next to leave. They've already stopped singing, and during the next several weeks will be flocking together in preparation for departure. Who can argue that nature, when left alone, paints some of the most beautiful scenes ever witnessed? Summer wildflowers constitute a palate of rich and vibrant colors that never fail to inspire feelings of awe and tranquility for those fortunate enough to view their glorious beauty. Butterfly weed is a common sight in dry, sunny spots.

White snakeroot flourishes in younger woods. Brilliant spikes of cardinal flower are frequent along streams and in wet woods. As spring fades into summer, spring ephemerals fade into memory. Perennials weave the thread of reliability and beauty in the garden after the early blooming flowers are gone. Summer is a time of beauty and abundance with summer blooming flowers in the garden. Though many summer flowering plants often suffer winter injury and require the tender care of spring, the color and fragrance of summer flowers adds brilliance and beauty in the garden. For flower lovers, hearts beat faster in summertime. By now, the new born of spring are fat and sassy basking in the heat and living off the abundance of the land.

Well into the growing season, it is a time to appreciate the present and anticipate the future. Fruit bearing native shrubs and trees such as chokecherry, American plum, and Juneberry attract birds and other wildlife. Vines such as riverbank grape produce a berry for wildlife and create nesting cover for birds. Fruit bearing plants attract waxwings, orioles, brown thrashers, gray catbirds, rufous-sided towhees, American robins, deer, grouse and pheasant. Huckleberries and other fruiting shrubs may show signs of being crushed under a bear's feet. All wild animals require three primary things: food, water, and shelter. Obviously, wildlife must have food to survive. Most wildlife can survive for weeks without food but only days without water. Cover is usually thought of as something animals hide under. Actually wildlife cover has two components: It provides shelter from adverse weather, and it provides protection from predators. Shrubs, thickets and brush piles provide great hiding places within their leaves, branches and thorns. Even dead trees work, as they are home to lots of different animals. Few things in life are as pleasant as sitting around a glowing fire on a warm summer night and gazing skyward at the tapestry of stars overhead. The cares of the day-to-day world can seem as distant as those flickering points of light. If you haven't stared at the night sky since winter you'll notice a big difference.

In the night sky, Deneb in Cygnus the swan, Altair in Aquila the eagle, and Vega in Lyra the harp make an almost perfect right triangle. The summer triangle is visible heralding summer just after sunset directly above you as you look straight up overhead. The Big and Little Dippers are clearly visible all night spinning around the pole star, Polaris. Since the earth's North Pole points to Polaris and the earth rotates around its poles, all the constellations seem to rotate around Polaris, including the Big Dipper. So the Big Dipper points to the North Star-it also points to other important stars-you can follow the Dipper's handle and "arc to Arcturus" , then "spike to Spica"- two very important stars. The Big Dipper and Little Dipper are always facing each other appearing as if something could be pouring out of the Little Dipper into the Big Dipper. If you are observing from a dark location far away from the bright city lights, you might notice a large hazy patch stretching clear across the sky. This hazy patch is the Milky Way, our galactic home. The hazy appearance is the result of hundreds of millions of stars packed so closely together that the light from the individual stars becomes indistinguishable. You may or may not agree that the winter sky is the more beautiful, but you will agree that no sky is more interesting than our summer sky.

It is then that the Milky Way is in its most favorable position for observation, for then, much of the brighter portion is in view with its numerous star clouds and various rifts, stretching as it does as a great band of light, arched from the southeast, high over the east point, and disappearing below the horizon near the north point. It's not enough to enjoy the most beautiful summer days, you've got to tap into the clear nights as well. Throughout the year, the cosmos puts on a terrific show after hours and for free, but summer is the best time to

Long-lasting daisy-like flowers atop purple coneflowers
appear in an unusual shade of mauve-purple
surrounding an iridescent red-orange, coned center.

take it all in. Summer skies display a wealth of interesting features. Butterflies abound in the wildflower-filled meadows. Meadowlarks and bobolinks nest in the low dense plant growth. With the passing of prime nesting season, the birds' melodic chorus is replaced by the buzz of the insect orchestra. There are signs that bird migration has quietly begun. Goldfinches pick at the seeds that form on the spent flowers of purple coneflowers. Somewhat pesty because of its colonizing tendency, butterfly bush holds high appeal to butterflies and hummingbirds as a popular nectar source. Monarchs find Mexican sunflower blossoms irresistible. The late season bloomers include grasses, asters, and goldenrods. The grassy meadows shine with color from the violet-purple flower rays of New England aster, the white flower heads of fleabane, and the yellow blooms of goldenrod. The late summer flowers thrive in the open fields in contrast to the grasses accompanying them.

The dry soil waits at the mercy of the clouds. Clouds, heavy with water spread out across the sky. When the water drops become too large for the rising air to hold them up, water falls as rain. Stems arch under the increased weight of water soaked leaves. Too much rain at one time places stress on strained stems. Too little rain and the water drops just run off the surface of the hard soil offering little relief to plants.

Rose of Sharon offers white, red, lavender, or light blue blooms when many flowering shrubs have long since ceased blooming. Alongside other perennials and grasses, tall stalks of Joe-Pye weed don fuzzy lavender flowers borne in flat-topped clusters. On a bright late summer day, purple flowers of ironweed glow. These are truly fall flowers and herald the coming of autumn. Dandelion can be found almost everywhere and blooms from April to November; in fact, it is sometimes found in the dead of winter. The hydrangea blooms have all lost their beautiful snowy shade, have turned green, and have begun to take on rosy hues as summer winds down. Memories of each bloom will lift the heart during the interlude between the peak of the growing season and the initiation of new life. In the months when summer transitions to fall,nature prepares for the coming changes by shedding what it no longer needs.

Summer is a wonderful time to wander around the woods. Trees are in leaf and flower with some providing a great nectar source for butterflies and bees.The leaves create a cooling shade and dappled sunlight filters through to the forest floor. Ferns unfurl their intricate fronds and are starting to spread out in the shadier parts of the woods. Watch as butterflies and bees glide from flower to flower in search of nectar. You may spot deer,foxes or squirrels.During the warmer months the woods are filled with a medley of color. Wildflower meadows sway in the warm breeze, the scent of fragrant honeysuckle fills the air and foxglove are filled with the buzzing of bees. You may see butterflies fluttering among the wildflowers and lots of activity from other insects.

The long days of summer bring about growth and ripening. Plants put forth fruit and seeds;young animals grow and learn. Summer is the time for plants and flowers to flourish and blossom. Warm weather and sunny days bring forth new growth and blooms. Summer typically is warm because during this time part of the earth is directly under the sun and its brilliant rays are focused on that part. Increased sunlight creates the perfect conditions for photosynthesis, the process by which plants transform light energy into chemical energy. Summer is the season of growth and maturation. Animals search out food, produce young, and store energy that will help them in the autumn and winter. Summer gives life,birth and rebirth to everything around us, plants bloom,animals resume activity and all of nature feels "alive" again.

Harvest

Blends of color create a breathtaking vision of a beautiful season. Colored chalk could not depict a finer picture. More colorful scenery could not be painted with brush on canvas. More intense shades could not be mixed on an artist's palette. A spectacle of color occurs each year at a time when the landscape is otherwise dull. Where a bud on a branch opens to expose a leaf, a drama unfolds. The cast of characters draws many to the wooded gallery. The forest trees, which transform cyclical, are changing colors. In order to retain moisture and survive the winter, trees stop producing chlorophyll. This is what causes leaves to lose their green color and turn yellow, gold and orange. When this happens, the carotenoid already in the leaves can finally show through. The leaves become a rainbow of glowing yellows, sparkling oranges and warm browns. As the trees prepare for winter, we see a fiery display of color. Autumn's a magic season, a time when much of the countryside erupts in a brilliant flash of red, orange, and yellow before fading away into the grays and whites of winter. Summer's heat and humidity has given way to cool, clear days. Fall is one of the greatest free shows on earth. Leaves show their true colors, hidden by chlorophyll, transforming the landscape into a riot of blazing colors, from parchment yellow to flaming gold, blush pink to roaring scarlet. Green lifeblood conceals that which was hidden beneath a veil of chlorophyll.

Shades of flame, saffron, and amber burst into view. A pageant of colors replaces bright green. As the days shorten and temperatures become cooler, the green of summer changes into a colorful palette of reds, oranges, golds, and browns before the leaves fall off the trees. As winter advances, trees in temperate and boreal zones face punishingly cold temperatures and frigid winds, conditions that would damage leaves, so trees have to reduce themselves to their toughest parts—stems, trunks, branches, bark. Leaves must fall off trees so that the tree can survive winter and grow new leaves in the spring. That's why every fall, deciduous trees get rid of their leaves and grow new ones in the spring. It's safer that way. Enjoy autumn's colorful farewell. Ultimately, the bright foliage will drop to give rise to dark silhouettes. Only a leaf scar will remain on the branch to indicate the spot where a leaf once was. The timber titans will tower above a more noticeable understory of shrubs and tangled vines. Vivid colors will fade. Hit by the fatal blow, the approach of winter becomes evident. Through winter's advance, the shiver may cut to the bone, but the heart will always be warm whenever autumn's dazzling color is recalled. The wind that warmed the flowers now chills the faded blooms. But, nature has one last fling before settling into winter's long sleep. The days get shorter and the temperature gets colder as winter nears. Autumn transforms right in front of our eyes from a showcase of color to bland stands of timber.

After the riot of color in autumn, with its brisk days, the still of winter sneaks up on us. During that time, animals forage heavily to build body fat. With seeds, nuts, and fruits at full bounty, animals scurry about eating as much as they can and storing more for later. Stockpiling food for winter is important when an animal's food source will soon be hidden by snow. Squirrels stash caches of mushrooms in the crotch of a branch, on top of a stump, or in the hollow cavity of a tree. Being off the ground helps the mushrooms to dry quickly and become tough and brittle. These dried mushrooms resist decay, unlike mushrooms still on the forest floor, and provide a meal for squirrels during the winter. In the ponds, bordered by stands of small trees, beavers cut and store cottonwood, aspen, and maple saplings so they can access them when the pond is frozen. For many animals, their food source is better left intact to be found as needed. Numerous berries stay on plants through winter and offer a food source to the first animal that finds them. Practically all wildlife species depend on plants for food and cover. White-tailed deer and cottontail rabbits depend on plants for food. Bobwhites, turkeys, and songbirds rely on plants for food and shelter. Plants are the fabric which covers the soil. They hold the soil in place and the soil holds everything they need. In addition to anchoring roots, soil provides life-sustaining water and nutrients. Whitetail bucks begin shedding their velvet.

The antlers are covered in velvet from the time that the antlers start growing in the spring, until the antlers stop growing in the late summer to early fall. When the antlers stop growing, they start to shed this velvet covering. In autumn an amazing transformation occurs that cuts the vital blood supply to the velvet. Soon thereafter, the "velvet" skin covering will crack and peel revealing polished antlers. Battered saplings bear the brunt of incessant rubbing and scraping of antlers. After rubbing off their velvet, over one day or a few days, bucks start to rub and play fight with trees and brush. During the fall, deer accumulate and store body fat under their skin and around internal organs. This serves both as insulation and energy reserve for the rigors of the winter ahead. Woodland residents seek out a sheltered, dry place where they will tranquilly sleep the cold winter away. Before an animal begins searching for that perfect site to hibernate, it spends most of its time either eating or assembling a food store to get it through the cold months ahead. Most of us live our lives without fear of becoming prey, without having to scavenge for or hunt and kill our food, and without having to learn to build a sturdy home or go without. In autumn, these challenges to animals become more apparent, as they prepare for winter, which is the most challenging time in the adult life of an animal in the wild. When you walk through the woods in autumn you may be very close to lots of sleeping animals. Just about all plants and many animals take the winter off.

They stop growing and just rest until spring. Many are heading south for the winter. The process of migration is complicated but made to appear simple by the millions of birds that take part every autumn (and again in the spring). Birds form groups and head south to better climates where they can live a bit easier while the north is under a blanket of snow and cold. Not all birds go south. Those that stay behind have plenty of their own work to do in order to ensure their survival. We do hear the buzzing of the chickadees and the rapping of the woodpeckers, but the lack of singing makes the forest seem empty and barren. Songbirds prepare for their annual voyage. Waterfowl migration is beginning. Rivers and open water, which formerly provided resting and feeding areas for ducks and geese, will soon be empty space. Great flocks will assemble to follow the starry constellations to faraway lands. Nonmigratory birds find refuge within the dense boughs of conifers growing in groves. Robins flock to pokeberries for a fall fruit feast. Robins prefer to remain year-round rather than seek cozier climes. They just are not always seen in winter because they tend to seek the shelter of dense thickets in cold weather. Monarch migration is underway. Winging along an ancestral roadmap that leads them on their way from south to north and back again these beautiful creatures traverse vast distances to reach their over wintering grounds on a regular round-trip ticket.

No single butterfly ever completes the entire trip rather freshly emerged generations hatched along the way take up the final leg of the trip to unseen ancestral wintering grounds two generations removed from the original travelers that began the trip. Nature is bringing many events together at one time to set off autumn's colorful changes. The changes start with the sun and the earth's orbit around it. The days get shorter and temperatures get colder as winter nears. Shorter days and cooler temperatures act as a signal to trees and plants to get ready for winter. All summer long, a tree's leaves have been making food for the tree so it can grow. In winter, the short days don't provide enough sunlight for the trees to make their food, so the trees live off the food they stored during the summer. Before winter arrives, the shorter days make the trees slow down their food making, and green chlorophyll disappears from the leaves. Like an artist mixes paint for his canvas, the chemicals mix to form different colors in different trees. Most perennials cannot withstand freezing temperatures for an extended length of time, so they go dormant during the coldest months. Perennial asters bloom in late autumn and begin to dry up. Even after the flowers or leaves are dead, the roots are still reclaiming energy from the dying plant for healthy growth in the spring.

The time for colorful blooms has come to pass for most flowers with the exception of a few plants that said "No" to fate by flowering during this unpredictable time of the year. Those that flowered and set seed have returned to the soil accomplishing their purpose. The day will come when the fall flowers will lose their color. Then, another season will have come and gone. Tired leaves do not indicate an end, but rather a beginning. As the days get shorter and the nights get longer and cooler, biochemical processes in the leaf paint the landscape with nature's autumn palette. Thoughts of leaf laden trees and flowering plants will lift the spirit during winter's melancholy. Dreams of fresh new growth pushing up through the soil will come true when the warmth returns. The blooms that brought joy, while they graced the landscape, will return. Green color starts to fade from leaves. Oaks turn red, brown, or russet; hickories, golden bronze; aspen and yellow-poplar, golden yellow; dogwood, purplish-red; beech, light tan; and sourwood and black tupelo, crimson. Maples differ species by species-red maple turns brilliant scarlet; sugar maple, orange-red; and black maple, glowing yellow. Leaves of some species such as the elms simply shrivel up and fall off, exhibiting little color other than drab brown. We all enjoy the colors of autumn leaves. Leaves are nature's food factories and they are simply gorgeous in their fall attire.

Rejoice in being alive as the flowers and the trees do and you'll know what it means to live for the day. A warm, sunny day in fall reminds us of a warm, sunny day in summer. Mild temperatures may tease the weatherglass, but the weather vane still points north. A new season has arrived that brings to culmination the events from seed to fruit. As the fall season trickles in, we each have a checklist to help us prep for winter. Just like us, trees take important steps to make sure they're ready for the new season. A tree can't depend on the fickle weather because it could be easily fooled by warm days that suddenly turn cold. Trees prepare for winter by shutting down nutrients to their leaves, a process that produces bursts of brilliant color in a final farewell. The time between the abundance of summer and the scarcity of winter represents the completion of a cycle which begins with life and ends with death. It is a time for gathering in before death's dark angel slays the living to yield the ghost. The time between extremes represents the culmination of all that has come to pass. Soon the teeth will chatter. The wind will blow through bare branches. Every year at this time we revel in the beauty of the trees, knowing full well that it is but a fleeting pleasure. Before long the leaves will flutter away from their summer homes to become part of the rich carpet of living soil that covers the forest floor. It is truly nature's bountiful gift, but you may not realize it. You might even think it's a nuisance!

Nature's autumn palette is painted on oaks, maples, beeches, sweetgums, yellow-poplars, dogwoods, hickories, and others. As the fall colors appear, other changes are taking place as well. At the base of the leafstalk, where it attaches to the twig, a layer of special cells develops and gradually severs the tissues that support the leaf. The damaged spot thereafter heals and all that is left behind is a leaf scar. For some, the coming of winter means permanent rest. For others, compensation for surviving the trials of life lies in the comforting arms of Morpheus. Seeds wait in seclusion for the return of the spring rains to lull them out of their winter haven. The rise of the mercury lifts the spirit, but first the inevitable must take place. A pale sun tries to break through the dismal clouds that block its light. The dreary clouds indicate change. Change is not always bad. It is change that tells the seed to germinate. It is change that tells the soil to accept the invitation. The dark shadows foretell what is to come. A gentle breeze now blows more forcefully. The sun waits for the clouds to scatter allowing its luminosity to shine down upon a landscape in transition. Sandwiched between blazing summer and chilly winter, autumn is the "cooling off" season. Nighttime arrives earlier, temperatures begin to drop and most vegetative growth decreases. Autumn is a time of transition and a time of preparation. Plants turn their attention from growth to harvest and nature herself prepares for winter sleep with a final flash.

The natural world is getting ready for the harshness of winter. Hearing and seeing flocks of birds gathering in the fields is a true sign of fall. Geese graze in the harvested corn and bean fields. Doves dine in the harvested soybean and wheat fields. As their name implies, wood ducks prefer bottomland forests, swamps, and freshwater marshes. Long before the autumn frosts have begun to close the northern ponds the wood duck has moved south towards its winter home in the rice fields, wooded sloughs, and the cypress swamps of the southern states mingling with the summer birds of these congenial climes. Hearing ducks or geese flying above your head, especially in the late fall, is an indication of winter coming. Many species of wildlife winter in marshes and swamps. In winter, a marsh may appear empty and windblown. It often seems a silent, frozen wilderness devoid of life and sound. Of course the ducks, geese, swallows, blackbirds, and shorebirds have flown south, but most earthbound creatures, even though we can't see or hear them, remain all winter long. Frogs, salamanders, and turtles disappear without a trace in the mud below the ice. Whatever the weather, each creature has its own response. Whether a species migrates, hibernates, adapts, or just survives as best it can. Warm-blooded animals can make their own heat to keep themselves warm, and they can burrow and hibernate to escape harsh conditions.

Annual plants die and leave their seeds to overwinter, usually under the snow or in the soil when conditions were more favorable. Perennial plants die back completely to the roots, and smaller woody perennials can overwinter under snowpack, protected and insulated. But trees are large, tall and immovable. They have no choice but to face everything winter can throw at them. The evergreen-pines, spruces, cedars, and so-on are able to survive winter because their needle-like or scale-like foliage is covered with a heavy wax coating and the fluid inside their cells contains substances that resist freezing. The leaves of broad leaved plants, on the other hand, are typically broad and thin and are not protected by any thick coverings. The fluid in the cells of these leaves is usually a thin, watery sap that freezes readily. With winter poised to make another grand entrance, every flower must close its colored petals. Energy used for cell maintenance and development is now used to just stay alive. Fruit, which contains seeds, represents the apex of existence in the plant Kingdom. It is not time to gather the sack cloth and ashes. Seeds formed this year will become plants that will bloom next year. Perennials wait beneath the copious soil for the much anticipated reunion. The winds of autumn are the winds of change. Enjoy the autumn festival of color. Majestic red tinted oaks and yellow, red, and orange colored maples seem to stretch out as far and as wide as the eyes can see.

Dazzling fall color brightens the towering trees and their accompanying understory companions. In woodlands where there are trees in various shades of yellow, brown, and orange and trees in shades of red and purple, the combination of fiery reds, golds, and bronzes can light up vistas, creating the typical autumn landscape so familiar in this natural wonderland. The season between the warmth of summer and the cold of winter adds contrast to a bare landscape. On a bright fall afternoon the shaded woods shine with colors. Every leaf in fall reveals its true color hidden beneath the green of summer. Every autumn, nature puts on a brilliant show of color. From bright yellows to vibrant reds, the leaves transform, showing their rich and radiant hues. Vividly colored fall leaves may grab your attention, but don't overlook the fall wildflowers which bloom in profusion along roadsides. A vase of fresh wildflowers is free and brightens any room. Trees have developed several adaptations that allow them to survive during the winter. The tree's bark acts as its first line of defence against the cold. In early autumn, in response to the shortening days and declining intensity of sunlight, leaves begin the process leading up to their fall. The veins that carry fluids into and out of the leaf gradually close off as a layer of cells forms at the base of each leaf.

Once this separation layer is complete and the connecting tissues are sealed off, the leaf is ready to fall. Leaves that fall are not wasted. They decompose and restock the soil with nutrients and make up part of the spongy humus layer of the forest floor that absorbs and holds rainfall. The peak of the white-tailed deer breeding season indicates that the fall flowers are not alone in dispersing their seed before winter. Branched antlers are carried by the bucks throughout most of the breeding season. After that the antlers are shed, and a new set begins to grow in spring. Their antlers drop off in late winter. A deer grows a new set of antlers by the following summer. Cabbage white butterflies take flight on warm afternoons in autumn even though the sun takes much longer to heat the ground. These dainty delights are sociable creatures that often enjoy the company of other whites and sulfurs at mud puddles. Butterflies tend to be slightly sluggish now. They usually are not real active until midday. Sunny, warm weather is best for butterflies. Those are the best conditions for these tiny winged wonders to take to the air for one more day of feeding. When night falls, butterflies fly off to seek secluded shelter for the evening under leaves, or in other protected areas. Most insects disappear during autumn but the invertebrates in the leaf litter carry on much as usual. Animals begin to prepare for the scarcity of food that generally comes during the winter, gathering stockpiles or going to warmer climates. Autumn is perhaps the best time to visit a woodland. Although there are not many flowers, the changing colors of the trees are very attractive. A more colorful picture cannot be painted by the most gifted painter of scenes. Color so vivid cannot be found in a paint mixing tray. More vibrant color cannot equal the humblest of the woodland trees in autumn. The painter of the autumn landscape brings together a canvas of blue with a backdrop of earthen tones. The autumn painting of leaves culminates when each tree stands bare in the forest without its leaves. Fallen leaves decompose in the soil restocking the top soil with nutrients. Leaves on the forest floor become food for numerous soil organisms vital to the forest ecosystem. It could well be that the forest could no more survive without its annual replenishment from leaves than the individual tree could survive without shedding these leaves. Although the trees appear inactive on the outside, they continue to be active on the inside. Water is drained from tender tissue to prevent damage done as a result of freezing. As the leaves fall off the twig, sap inside thickens and congeals into syrupy "antifreeze". Eons of evolution have resulted in survival strategies to help deciduous trees stay alive in the winter. Dark silhouettes lend an eerie elegance to the woods in winter.

Trees may go dormant going into winter, but the distinctive beauty of their bare branches complementing a gray sky in winter serves to remind us that they continue to regulate metabolic processes and physiological activities only at a slower rate. A tree heading towards winter will sense the changing temperature and light duration and obey dormancy controls built into the leaf. The "Indian summer" days of autumn, when the days are clear and sunny and the nights are cool and crisp, provide an almost irresistible lure to those who enjoy the outdoors. Roadside views of forests in autumn stir up excitement. Trails winding deep into forest solitude offer a special closeness to nature. The quiet surfaces of forest lakes double the mantle of surrounding hills. Mist-filled valleys provide a colorful backdrop for placid lake waters that reflect the soft medley of fall foliage. Scientists don't fully understand all the complicated actions -and even more complicated interactions-involving pigments, sunlight, moisture, chemicals, temperature, length of daylight, genetic traits, and so on that make for a spectacular show of autumn colors. But full understanding is not necessary to the enjoyment of the lovely days of autumn. As the fall color season gradually comes to an end, some pockets of color are still noticeable. Although the leaves are falling, they reveal in their decline and fall last summer's results and next spring's promise. As the winter solstice nears, hardwood trees are mostly bare, stark against the sky, without their leaves.

With their leaves gone, the trees are ready to take on winter's slings and arrows. The sunny days of summer last only in memory. A landscape once cloaked in bright color now wears more somber tones. As the days grow shorter and colder, those changes trigger a hormone in leaf-dropping trees that sends a chemical message to every leaf that says, in essence, "Time to go! " Saying goodbye to summer is made more tolerable by the beauty of fall color. The last of the annual flowers rejoice in their final hour. Having sown the seeds of their succession they have arrived at their purpose. Annuals are among the most adaptable of flowering plants. Annuals come up in the spring, grow, flower, set seed, then die after the first frosts in fall. The perennials prepare for dormancy. They retreat underground anticipating winter. Many perennials that are left standing provide a nutritious source of seed for wildlife. Some birds find the abundance left behind by these perennials particularly tasty. The upright stems of perennials offer a place to hide in winter. The chill in the air suggests a change is coming. A few hardy wildflowers flourish even now as autumn reaches its stunning peak. New England asters bloom in the damp thickets and transitional meadows. Purple rays surround a yellow disk. It is amazing how the fall wildflowers seem to match the upcoming fall tree colors, particularly the central disks of the asters.

Trails winding deep into forest solitude
offer a special closeness to nature.

Prolific flowers late in the year coincide nicely with the monarch migration.

Flowers are a beautiful part of the life cycle of seed-producing plants. The beautiful Baltimore checkerspot butterfly caterpillar relies exclusively on the unique flower of white turtlehead which, as its name implies, resembles a turtle's head. For each type of butterfly, its larva (caterpillar) can only feed on specific plant species. These specific plant species are referred to as butterfly host plants. One larva's staple is another one's poison. Joe Pye weed is not used as a caterpillar food source but its large flower clusters provide nectar for butterflies. After flowering, its bronze colored seed heads persist into winter. Brightly colored butterfly weed is a butterfly magnet. Monarchs like this plant twice as much since it is both a nectar source and a host plant for their caterpillars. The colors of wildflowers attract birds and insects, and through this attraction, plants are pollinated and seeds are dispersed. People also are attracted to wildflowers. We seek the natural beauty of wildflowers to brighten our days. Now we must wait for the spring sun to warm the forest floor and coax the trillium, Dutchman's breeches, bloodroot, phlox and other "spring ephemerals" to appear. Juicy, red berries ripen upon the branches of autumn olive. Although its edible berries are eaten by birds, raccoons, skunks, and opossums, autumn olive is non-native and can aggressively outcompete our native plants and shrubs. Black walnut trees produce fruit in the form of a nut, borne singly or in pairs, enclosed in a solid, non-splitting green husk.

Large quantities of these nuts are distributed by the tree, then collected and buried by squirrels. Later most hidden nuts will be relocated as needed by its own fragrance. All trees and shrubs produce some type of fruit. The type of fruit varies greatly, but many wildlife species depend on mast as an important source of food in their diet. Mast is typically categorized as either soft or hard. Hard mast consists of hard shelled seeds that have a relatively long shelf life and are typically high in fat, carbohydrates, and protein. These characteristics make them a food source that is both high in energy content and available well into the winter months. Soft mast is fleshy, perishable fruit that is often high in sugar, vitamins, and carbohydrates. It is usually not available in large quantities during the winter months. Soft mast can be an important energy source for some wildlife species during migration. All living things need food to survive, so food sources are a critical component of wildlife habitat. Plants form the foundation of the food chain in the natural world. Plants provide food to wildlife in a variety of ways, from berries to nuts and even the insects that they provide for. Even dead trees play a part by being a magnet for insects, mosses, lichens and fungi, this deadwood becomes a cafeteria for wildlife looking for a snack. Wildlife have high food requirements in spring and summer-not only do they have themselves to feed but their offspring, too. In winter, it's worse.

Migration is probably the riskiest activity birds undertake in their lives, in spite of that, every year thousands of birds make long journeys around the globe, moving from areas of declining resources to areas of abundant resources. And, these birds fly hundreds of thousands of miles in the process, which is an insane feat of endurance. Spring migration gets more attention, but fall migration lasts longer-almost half the year-and involves more birds, since surviving adults are joined by young birds hatched during the summer. Birds do not have calendars, however, they rely on different factors to determine when fall begins and it is time for migration, and they use different cues to determine when the time is right to move from their breeding range to their wintering range. By August, nesting season has ended. For many people, it's the end of vacation season. While human families begin returning to work and starting school, birds begin flocking in preparation for fall migration. The energy once put into preparing nestlings for independence is now spent growing new feathers for the journey. The success of annual migration for songbirds is affected by the quality of habitat at stopover sites, particularly in relationship to food needed for rapid refueling, These safe places where birds can rest and refuel along their migration routes in order to maintain their health and continue their journey are where songbirds spend most of their time and energy during this crucial time for birds.

The quality of suitable stopover sites depends on the abundance and nutritional quality of food resources linked to the presence of deciduous shrubs that provide seasonal fruit in the fall and support insects in the spring. When migrating songbirds fail to find sufficient food at stopover sites, their migratory flights are delayed, or worse. Those that do arrive at their breeding and wintering grounds, often arrive late and in poor physical condition, and are forced to select poor quality habitat for nesting, resulting in decreased nesting success and reduced survival rates. Migratory birds often stop along their long journeys to replenish their fat stores. The purpose of these stopovers- rest and refueling- is clear. Bright colors and falling leaves , as well as other less obvious changes in the tree, are due to biochemical reactions triggered by autumn's shortening day length and cool-but not freezing-temperatures. With declining autumn temperatures, tree leaves stop producing chlorophyll, the green pigment of photosynthesis. The color of a tree's fall foliage depends on the combination of pigments in the leaves. The leaves of trees in summer are characteristically green because of the presence of chlorophylls that dominate and mask out the colors of any other pigments that may be present in the leaf. Carotenoids give us colorations of yellow, brown, orange and many hues in between.

Their brilliant yellows and oranges tint the leaves of such hardwood species as hickories, ash, maple, yellow-poplar, aspen, birch, black cherry, sycamore, cottonwood, sassafras, and alder. The reds, purples, and their blended combinations that decorate autumn foliage come from another group of pigments called anthocyanins. In our autumn forests, they show up vividly in the maples, oaks, sourwood, sweet gum, dogwood, tupelo, black gum, and persimmon. While all trees contain the yellow carotenoid pigments, not all possess the genetic potential for producing anthocyanins, which cause the pink, red, and purple leaf colors. Like the carotenoids, anthocyanins are unmasked when autumn temperatures halt the leaves' production of chlorophyll. While trees are responding to the cooler temperatures, they are also reacting to the shorter day lengths of autumn. As the duration of night increases, the cells near the juncture of the leaf and the stem begin to divide rapidly, but they do not expand. A corky layer of cells forms that slowly begins to block the transport of materials such as carbohydrates from the leaf to the branch, causing leaf fall. It also blocks the flow of minerals from the roots into the leaves. Despite the traditional belief, weather plays no role. The trees possess an inner clock which is triggered by the length of the daylight.

Because the starting time of the whole process is dependent on night length, fall colors appear at about the same time each year at a given location, regardless of whether temperatures are cooler or warmer than normal. The sun's light disappears a little earlier in the evening than it did during the summer. Its bright light begins to show a little later in the morning than it did during the summer. Fall flowers remind us of summer's blooms. Bright color is reduced to dull shades. The flowers of fall are worth waiting all summer for. The flash of asters, the bright spark of goldenrods, and the richness of chrysanthemums push the garden to a crescendo of color even as the days grow shorter. Summer flowers fade as frost begins to nip the garden, but pansies, dianthus, and their cool-season companions keep right on blooming while the trees above are putting on their spectacular autumn show. A garden full of fall flowers will also be alive with butterflies. Although we see butterflies mostly in the spring and summer, it is important to remember that many still have a need for nectar sources in the fall. Monarchs migrate thousands of miles and need good nectar sources along the way to successfully arrive at their over wintering sites in Mexico and southern California. Even butterflies that don't migrate could use extra nourishment in fall. Many butterflies over winter in various life stages.

Some over winter as eggs, and the adults that lay them need that extra nutritional boost at the end of the season to produce large numbers of healthy eggs that can withstand the winter. Coneflowers will be finishing their intense cycle of bloom, but goldfinches and chickadees perch on their handsome seed heads and help themselves. Especially in fall, migrating birds, as well as those that spend the winter in your garden, will enjoy the seeds and berries your trees, shrubs, and flowers have produced during the mild spring and summer. When autumn goes away another change takes place which will affect everything alive. September's dawn hesitates with each new morning, weary perhaps from the busyness of summer's unceasing activity. The long daylight hours are filled with a multitude of treasured moments to remember throughout winter's dark freeze. Cooler nights and shortened days herald the transition of seasons and prepare us to embrace the change. It is wet and grey more often than not as winter pushes its way in bringing on the end of autumn.

There are new stars in the autumn sky. In the northern hemi-sphere Cassiopeia, Pegasus, and Cygnus grace the night sky. As the warm nights of summer give way to crisp autumn evenings, the changing seasons bring many changes to the night sky as the Summer Triangle which has dominated overhead for several months now begins to sink lower in the west, to be replaced in its lofty position by Andromeda and Pegasus, which first become visible just after dark in the east to northeast.

At this time of year, the earth is facing out into space. This gives us a good chance to see The Andromeda Galaxy, our nearest galaxy neighbor. In the southern night sky during the late-evening the zodiac constellations of Aquarius, Capricornus, and Pisces can be seen in a region of the heavens known as the "Celestial Sea" because of the watery themed constellations that are found there. On a clear, moonless night, step outside and look up at the sky. Stars millions of light years away, galaxies and nebulas- the night sky provides enough detail to keep the mind wandering for hours. People have been doing this for thousands of years. They spent hours looking at the night sky. They found that by connecting the stars as if they were dots, patterns emerged that resembled animals, people and things. Today, we call these star patterns constellations. Many of the striking star groups and our beautiful Milky Way galaxy, which made for great stargazing on balmy summer evenings, are still visible in the western sky. Thanks to a quirk of Earth's axial tilt, we get the chance to view astronomical summer jewels, catch autumn gems at their finest and take the first glimpses of the delights of winter. Autumn is a season of promise for viewing the stars, constellations, planets and much more. The nights are getting longer, the air clearer, and those pesky mosquitoes are a thing of the past. But, the appearance now of the brilliant star Capella ascending above the northeast horizon in the evening hours is a promise of the chillier nights to come.

In a few months the constellation Orion and his neighbors will be dominating the evening skies, providing a celestial marker for the chilly winter season ahead. Deciduous trees delight our eyes with brilliant colors of golds, oranges, and reds. Length of daylight and chemicals in leaves are behind why leaves change colors. We know autumn is here when the bright green summer landscape changes to reveal brilliant reds, oranges, yellows, and golds. But leaves are not on trees just to make them pretty. Trees need leaves to keep them alive! Conifers or evergreen trees remain green throughout the year and drop their needles mainly in the spring. Many animals begin their migration to milder temperatures and steadier food supply. Some animals pass the cold months in a sort of suspended animation called hibernation. Many insects die as the colder weather of winter approaches. Some insects dig deep into the ground. Other insects hibernate in the egg, larval or pupal stage. Some butterflies migrate to warmer climates. An abundant acorn crop means that chipmunks, mice, rabbits, and squirrels are busy harvesting as many acorns as possible before winter. If the little guys are well fed, the winter will be a good season for predators such as owls, red-tailed hawks, foxes, and coyotes, too. Watch out for chubby squirrels scampering around adding to their nut stores. In autumn, the woods are alive with lavish displays of color, arching antlers of agile bucks, and the last faded leaves floating gently downstream as wild geese call out overhead.

In winter, all life seems seeped out. The chorus of frogs,

insects and birds has fallen silent; the only sound is the roaming wind in the barren treetops. Even the sunlight seems weakened, as if the year of life and renewal and beauty has left all of creation too tired to do anything but sleep and dream of what once was. One of the most beautiful transitions is from winter to spring. From the quiet solitude and depth of winter, flowers bloom, trees leaf out, birds build nests and animals awaken. As winter bids farewell and the days start warming and brightening, you start to feel your mood improve, as you become less weighed down by the cold and dreary days of winter. Remembering spring's colorful flowers serves as an antidote to the gloom of winter,offering us color when we need it most.

A visit to the woods during this amazing season is always a treat. This time of year is perfect for watching wildlife. You can watch the deparure of migrant birds,see the spectacle of deer rutting, admire intricate spider webs as they appear and look out for foraging squirrels in search of nuts. Being in the woods in autumn can sometimes be a little over whelming. Mother Nature puts on such a grand show that it is difficult to know where to look first. There is color everywhere, from the tops of the trees that are still retaining their leaves to the forest floor carpeted with the multicolored leaves that have let go. The sounds in the woods in autumn are mesmerizing. The rustling of leaves underfoot, the snap of twigs and branches hiding under the carpet of leaves, or the trees creaking in the wind. The caw of a crow, the jeer of a blue jay, or the hoarse screech of a red-shouldered hawk (which might in fact be a blue jay mimicking a red-shouldered hawk).

Departure

A layer of moist leaves covers the ground. Leaves, in a variety of shapes and sizes, create a kaleidoscopic view. A patchwork of yellow, red, and brown stands out against faded blades. Broken blisters hurt until the skin hardens to numb the pain. Calloused hands should not harden the heart. Each fallen leaf will be broken down by soil microbes and become one with the soil. Trees add to the organic matter in soil as they lose their branches and leaves. Each individual tree itself will ultimately contribute to the humus when it dies, decomposes, and breaks down. Every handful of soil contains a wealth of biological riches hidden from view. These microorganisms break down dead plants and animals extracting nutrients that plants need to grow. Plants absorb these nutrients from the soil through their roots. Then they return the nutrients to the soil when they die or lose branches and leaves. New plants then absorb the nutrients from the soil and start the cycle over again. A philosophers' stone is not needed to create gold. Living soil is more precious than gilded metal. Basically, soil is made as living things die, the matter starts to decay, and this breaks into tiny bits and mixes through natural processes such as rain and wind. Under the ground beneath your feet is a whole world of life forms that are going about their daily activities. An array of organisms aerate, mix, and add nutrients to the soil. Aerated soil allows water to penetrate more deeply. The mixed in soil sustains green plants. Thirsty roots take up nutrients dissolved in water from the soil. Soil organisms feed on the ambrosia. The effects of rain, snow, freezing, and thawing break down rock, soil, and minerals into micro components that can be readily used by plants. The fragmented rock forms the skeletal material of soil. The forces of wind and water, heat and cold, grind down rock and organic matter like a pestle and mortar. Most plants get their nutrients from the soil and they are the main source of food for humans, animals and birds. And so, most living things on land depend on soil for their existence. Through phototropic alignment of the leaf and making use of organic matter directly from the soil new leaves use the power of the sun to transform sunlight into energy. The primary source of energy for nearly all life is the sun. Not all of the light from the sun makes it to the surface of the earth. Even the light that does make it here is reflected and spread out. The little light that does make it here is enough for plants to survive and go through the process of photosynthesis. The energy that drives photosynthesis originates in the center of the sun, where mass is converted to heat by the fusion of hydrogen. Over time, the heat energy reaches the earth's surface, where some of it is converted to light by black body radiation that reaches the earth. A small fraction of the visible light coming in contact with the earth's surface is absorbed by plants. Light is actually energy, electromagnetic energy to be exact.

When that energy gets to a green plant, all sorts of reactions occur to store that energy in the form of sugar molecules. Chlorophyll is the magic compound that can grab that sunlight and start the whole process. Chlorophyll is found in the chloroplasts,which are organelles most abundant in leaf cells. Photosynthesis happens in the chloroplasts. Chlorophyll is the green coloring in leaves that traps light energy from the sun, which is then used to combine carbon dioxide and water into sugars in the process of photosynthesis. Plants need nutrients from the soil to grow, just as we need food. Soil nutrients come from the breakdown of mineral-bearing rocks and from organic matter, which comes from the decomposition of plants and animals. The nutrients that plants get from the soil are stored in plant tissues, such as leaves, stems, and flowers. When these plant tissues fall to the ground they start to break down, and together with decomposing dead insects and dead animals, they eventually re-incorporate into the soil. Leaves that find final repose upon the bare ground were very important for the tree – they provided food for the whole tree. Nutrients used by the tree for its own very special processes are released back into the soil from which it was only temporarily borrowed. It is a delight to visit the deciduous woodlands at any time of the year, and during winter is no exception. Trees in winter are especially attractive. In this season of pause before new growth, skeleton trees have stark beauty.

Massive smooth, silver-grey trunks are the most striking feature in beech woods. The oak tree has an enormous trunk with curled branches. The ash tree has a smoother outline. The maple's outer branches make the tree appear egg-shaped. The branches of the elm make the tree look like an inverted cone. Basswood often grow in clumps on the fertile floodplains. Trees are biologically engineered to adjust to most of the things "Mother Nature" dishes up. Unlike animals, trees cannot move. Unlike many other plants, they don't have the option to overwinter as seeds or rhizomes, so they must rely on physiological and structural adaptations. The height of trees, a benefit during the summer, becomes a liability in winter, as tissues are exposed to the weather. Bark provides a fairly tight barrier to water loss for most tree tissues. The bark also helps protect the tissues from abrasion and any physical damage. However, broad leaves are a major source of water loss, so our northern deciduous trees drop them in the fall. Conifers needles have proportionately less surface area than leaves and also have better water loss control barriers. Conifers have an advantage in needle retention in that they can photosynthesize all year, as conditions permit. The somber interval cloaks the landscape in black and white. Sunshine glistening on the snow covered ground reflects like a glass mirror reminiscent of the warmth that tells the seed to awaken.

The chilling beauty and desert-like stillness of winter draws us outdoors and offers a fresh new prospective. Soon the trees will be completely bare of leaves. Frosty mornings cause trees to glisten in the first light. Bright sunlight glimmers on frosted leaves making you tingle with a feeling of being really alive. Winter is a challenging time for all living things, including trees. Trees go through a process similar to hibernation called dormancy, and that's what keeps them alive during the winter. Winter is a certainty that all perennial plants must face each year. The number of hours of daylight is shorter so there is less sunlight in winter. Without sunlight green plants cannot photosynthesize and make their food. The cold temperatures of winter slow them down and stops their growth. Like animals, some plants survive winter in resting stages. Many perennials lose the parts of themselves that are exposed as the temperature drops. The roots in the ground move as much of the water in their tissue's cells into the surrounding ground as possible. With less moisture in the plant's cells, a certain amount of freezing and thawing can occur without rupturing those cells. Also, sugars and salts in the roots act as a natural antifreeze. By lowering the freezing point of the water in the plant's cells, it allows them to survive lower temperatures. Annuals live for one year. It is the seeds of annuals that survive through winter.

Many annuals are prolific producers of seeds, ensuring that at least some will be in the right place at the right time, usually in spring. Favorable conditions include not just soil temperature and texture but also moisture and light. Trees have to survive all winter with their trunks and branches above ground all winter, exposed to the cold, freezing wind and snow. Just like seeds and the root-storage organs, the buds of trees, which contain next year's leaves, can "tell" when winter has passed and spring has arrived. Snowmelt and early rains influence the growth of leaf buds on tree branches. As temperatures rise and rainfall increases, these buds grow to be leaves. Winter buds are usually well protected by scales, pubescence, or a resinous layer. Winter is the most stressful time of the year for most forms of life. The main hardships are lack of food and cold temperatures. A lack of food occurs for two reasons, both related to cold temperatures. The first has to do with a reduction in active plant life. Plants are the base source of nearly all food chains. The second has to do with availability of food. Many food sources are buried under snow and ice. When the leaves begin to fall and winter starts to creep in, we're usually so concerned with our own needs that it's easy to forget all the animals and insects left outside to fend for themselves. Snow cover and cold temperatures can affect overwintering insect survival rates. Light fluffy snow provides more insulation than packed snow.

Insects that overwinter in the egg stage often survive colder temperatures better than insects in other growth stages. In order to survive winter, insects push the pause button, actually the diapause button. The shorter daylight lengths of fall trigger insects to enter diapause. In order for insects to continue to the next life stage, diapause has to be terminated. The" play button" is usually warmer temperatures. The trees are bare making it much easier to watch seldom-seen wildlife. Everything living and non- living stands out in contrast against a hushed, snow-white backdrop-conditions that make most animals that much easier to spot. Hawks are establishing their winter hunting territories. Roadside raptors wait in silent ambush for their prey. Only a lucky white-footed mouse can escape the sharp talons of a swooping red-tailed hawk on the wing. The silent flight, mournful calls and nocturnal behavior of owls makes them both magical and mysterious. A fair mimic will likely receive a response. A great-horned owls hoot, like a coyote's howl, is a classic sound of the wild and can be heard a long way off. River otters forage along stream bottoms for winter-chilled frogs, crayfish, and fishes. Playful and carefree otters toboggan down snowy hills into rivers. Otters slide for an obvious reason: Fun. The sight of woodlands coated in snow is one of winter's most magical images. Tracks in the snow are some of the easiest to read. Animals and plants face stress at this time of year, too.

Unlike the psychological stress we bring upon ourselves, their stress is largely physiological. A cycle has come full circle. Even the most resilient plants are pushed to their limit. Isolated confinement is the price paid by plants that return. The warmth of spring will be their liberation. They wait for the wintry weather to wind down, hidden in the darkness of their soil refuge, for the gentle nudge of spring to persuade them to return above ground. The coldness will be more than the delicate plants can endure. Abandoned,winter takes its toll. Iced up tender tissue results in death and decay. The sky seems a deeper blue in winter. In the summer it is a milky washed-out blue, which in winter becomes a richer, deeper and darker shade of blue. Even the stars seem a little brighter in winter. The bitter chill of a clear winter night is compensated by the brilliance of the starry sky above. The luster of the night sky containing the beautiful wintertime constellations is seemingly nature's holiday decoration to celebrate the winter solstice and enlighten the long cold nights of winter. Bright lights illuminate the night sky. Each star shines like a sparkling diamond in the sky. The jewels of the night sky unite to form "pictures" in the sky. The clear night sky is filled with an amazing assortment of characters and creatures. Winter is the season of Orion, the hunter. Orion shines like a gigantic piece of celestial jewelry through the frosty winter air. The twins are companions of Orion in the winter sky.

On a dark and clear moonless night, look for the soft- glowing river of stars that we call the Milky Way to meander right through the Winter Circle. The brightest star we can see in the winter sky at night is Sirius in Canis Major, the big dog. Moving northward and clockwise in the sky we can see Procyon in Canis Minor, the little dog. Moving further northward we encounter the Gemini twins, Pollux and Castor. Now we swing up and over to a constellation almost directly over-head-Auriga. Continue to swing southward in the sky until we arrive at the bottom right star representing Orion's left foot. We complete the Winter Circle by swinging back to Sirius. Following the age old paths seen in the heavens we move through the seasons. Curiosity and awe lead the way. Discoveries are made, insights flow, and our horizons expand. The days are usually clouded during this weary season, but the nights are usually clear allowing an unobstructed view of an airy expanse filled with stars, the moon, and the planets. One reason for the clarity of a winter's night is that cold air cannot hold as much moisture as warm air can. Hence, a warm moisture- laden night in the summer causes the sky to appear hazier. During winter, Mother Nature herself offers the sky observer in north temperate latitudes the two gifts of longest nights and a sky more transparent than usual. The cold reminds us that the warmth of spring is far away. The return of new growth will be delayed until the soil is warmed by a renewed sun. Bright colors have faded.

The bare trees are icy and unadorned. Some animals hibernate (go into a deep sleep) so they can survive the cold season. Plants that survive winter will return in the spring and summer to once again beautify the landscape. Plants that complete their life cycle in a single season will die away with the decreasing sunlight. Sources of new life have been sown. They remain in the soil seed bank, waiting to germinate. Plants lose water through their leaves by a process called transpiration. Apart from the problem of a shortage of available water during the winter, photosynthesis would be difficult because there are only a few hours of very weak sunlight. Deciduous trees such as oaks, ash, and beech shed their leaves in autumn. On cold winter days, the water in the soil is frozen, so it cannot be taken up by the roots, the air temperature may be quite warm if the sun is shining, and so if leaves were still on the trees they would lose a lot of water and wilt. This would result in the death of the tree. So dropping the leaves before winter sets in is the most sensible thing a deciduous tree can do! Birds are lucky in being able to fly and at the end of summer, when the days are getting shorter and food more scarce, some species fly off to a warmer climate. Snakes, lizards, frogs, toads, and newts slow down all their body processes almost to a stop in very cold weather. This is known as diapause and in this state the animals use up just a small amount of their store of body fat and can survive for some weeks, barely alive.

Many invertebrates hide themselves away too. Some adult insects die at the end of summer but their eggs, larvae or pupae spend the winter hidden away, ready to begin again when spring comes. The weather vane will spin round on a south wind. The fallen leaves and the faded flowers will grow anew perfecting lush, green, picture-perfect plants. A bright sphere will take its place in the heavens illuminating a deep blue sky. The luminaries will realign to usher in a brand new season. Until then the silver-footed queen of the night will rule sovereign. The heat of the brilliant flame surrenders to the cold north wind. Most living things seek shelter from the cold. Birds and animals deal with the arrival of winter in different ways. Some opt to migrate to warmer or more favorable climates. Other animals go into hibernation, and still others adapt and tough it out. Overwintering animals that do occasionally wake up at intervals to venture out on warmer days find that a winter wonderland holds many secrets. Unique sights and sounds enhance a magical season. Autumn is a time of preparation for mammals. They fatten themselves up by eating as much as possible. Smaller mammals lose heat more quickly than larger ones and so they must burn up their fat fast to keep warm. This is why mice and voles make themselves cozy, underground nests during the winter. Foxes and deer can remain active throughout the winter because of their larger size.

The mammals that find it most difficult of all to cope in the winter are those which rely mainly on invertebrates for their food. Most invertebrates are hard to find in the winter. The only way insectivorous mammals can survive is to slow their body processes to almost a stand still-they do this by hibernating. All summer, with long hours of sunlight and a good supply of liquid water, plants are busy making and storing food, and growing. In winter, the days are much shorter, and water is hard to get. Annuals complete their life cycle in one growing season. They die when winter comes, but their seeds remain, ready to sprout again in the spring. Perennials survive for many years. They are either herbaceous plants with soft, fleshy stems or woody like trees and shrubs. The above ground parts of herbaceous plants (leaves, stems) die off, but the underground parts (roots, bulbs) remain alive. Trees and shrubs begin to harden- off - that is, develop cold tolerance in response to the shorter days and cooler temperatures of early fall. While shoot growth has stopped for the year, roots continue to grow until the soil freezes in winter. In winter, plants rest and live off stored food until spring. Forests contain birds that never learned to migrate. Instead, they choose to remain behind expressing a message of hope with each cheerful chirp. Birds are the flowers of our winter gardens. What a great delight it is to watch the activity in our own backyards. Winter, however, probably provides less entertainment for the birds as it does for us.

The tiny songsters walk a fine line between life and death as they continually labor to gain food, water, and living space. Cold temperatures are survivable by most birds. How can something so small and fragile possibly survive such brutally cold conditions? Like us, they often try to find places that are well protected from wind and "cold air". While birds can't put on an extra set of feathers in cold conditions, they can fluff up. Normally, birds that you see in the trees, in woods, or in your backyard are ones that stick around during the winter in your climate. These winter birds have a better chance of maintaining their territory year-round, and they avoid the hazards of migration. But in exchange they have to endure the cold. It all starts in late summer and early fall. Some birds leave their summer home to find a new place with warmer temperatures. Other birds find ways to adapt to changing weather. Birds do a lot of things in winter, but their main focus is finding food and staying warm. Winter weather with its ice, strong winds, and heavy wet snow can present a challenge to survival for birds and other wildlife. On the whole, assume that the birds you do see in winter are usually well adapted to withstand the heavy hand of normal winter weather. Cold temperatures don't hurt most birds- as long as they have food. They store fat during the short days of winter to keep themselves warm during the long nights. During those freezing nights, they fluff their feathers to trap heat and slow their metabolism to conserve energy.

You may see birds outside fluffed up, trapping air in their down feathers, creating their own "down coats", so to speak. The down feathers insulate the birds, keeping the heat of their bodies inside. They make their own body heat by shivering; as long as they have food to give them energy, they can survive extreme cold. Millions of years of evolution have contributed to brave birds learning to survive winter and winter residents learning to adapt to the available food. The first snowfall of the year is considered a special event, but it usually melts quite quickly. Different animals react differently to harsh conditions, some even thrive under these circumstances, but for others, the longer the snow stays around, the more animals will die. Lingering cold and snow not melting can be difficult on sensitive species such as quail. Quails are ground feeders that live on seeds. When they can't reach the ground, they starve. Birds are like little furnaces. The real danger is when they run out of fuel for the furnace. For squirrels, this is a delicate time: the heart of their first mating season, which usually is from the last week in January through the first few weeks of February. This is the time of year they're feeling frisky. Squirrels, like quails, are most affected by prolonged snow cover and the inability to find their widely dispersed, buried food caches. Not all animals suffer in the snow. Mice, shrews, and voles do well beneath the snow in insulated areas and tunnels left in the vegetation now covered by snow.

Heat rises from the earth and is captured by the snow, keeping the temperature in this area, called the subnivean zone, close to freezing, even if the temperature above is in single digits. It can be a difference of 20 or 30 degrees, which can be the difference between life and death. Reptiles, amphibians, and many mammals hibernate. Some species tough it out. Deer walk a thin survival line in winter, especially when we get to late February and early March. Fawns have a hard time in winter. Many of them will die as the adult does push them away from food in order to survive themselves. A two year old doe is best prepared to survive a grueling winter. Turkeys also struggle when we have snow cover. After a big winter storm, snow gets too deep to scratch through for food. Wildlife do not have the option of staring out the window hoping for spring's arrival; unless they are of the type that hibernates. The rest are left to make do. They try to maintain body temperature by seeking the shelter of trees, brush, and snow banks. Pale leaves lie, on top of tired blades of grass, covered by snow. Each leaf, at first glance giving the impression of little worth, crosses over into the most useful phase of its life cycle. Each detached leaf is what was. Its final repose becomes what will be. Rather than representing an end, the fallen leaves represent a beginning. It's common knowledge that trees become bare during winter, but not many people actually know how they keep themselves alive during the bitter cold of winter.

Trees don't sleep through the winter. They struggle to survive, just like all other living things that must endure the trials of winter. Winter's heavy snow and ice, as well as frozen soil, can cause damage to trees and shrubs. Branches of trees can break due to excessive weight of ice and snow. Winter winds can cause evergreens to lose moisture from their needles. Deciduous trees suffer from winter drying. Long ago in the fossil forests long vanished the original trees must have died off in extremely large numbers in response to the very first change of seasons. Eventually a few determined, vigorous individuals developed ways to cope with the changes passing on their effectiveness to their successors via the seed. Woody plants evolved that could endure the drastic alteration of climatic conditions. A new and improved perennial developed that could prosper despite the stress caused by the effects of freezing and thawing. A hardened outer covering around its stem improved the plant's ability to remain alive while still being exposed to the harshness of the elements. It was no longer necessary to retreat back into the soil where the plant remained alive as root stock until the arrival of spring. Winter could be faced head on and the plant would still survive to boast of the confrontation. Freezing temperatures are a certainty that all plants must face each year. Protective membranes developed to foster preservation of tender buds and vulnerable exposed leaf scars.

Stems, twigs, and buds are equipped to survive severe extreme cold so that they can reawaken when spring returns. As a result, woody perennials evolved safeguards for self-preservation permitting them to survive the change of seasons. All deciduous trees lose their leaves and go into a dormant state. Many animals also go dormant through the winter. As the Earth, tilted on its axis, travels in a loop around the Sun each year the seasons change. Each morning the sun rises a little later and dips a little lower in the sky. The shorter days of fall send a signal to every living thing in the forest. Winter is coming! The cold causes living things all sorts of problems. Freezing temperatures turn water into ice so that animals cannot drink, and plants cannot take up water through their roots to enable them to make food (the process known as photosynthesis).When winter comes, woodchucks move into underground dens and begin a deep sleep. Soon the woodchuck's heart slows and its body temperature drops. For months it will not eat or drink. Bears and skunks take long naps too, but their heart rates and temperatures stay close to normal. Their winter fat helps feed them and keep them warm. Cold -blooded animals—turtles, snakes, toads, and insects keep warm and alive under the ground, where they sleep until spring comes. Moles dig down below the frost line and stay active, feeding on worms and insects they find in their tunnels. Shrews have little time to rest in winter.

These tiny mouse-like animals must eat almost constantly-day and night! - Just to stay alive. They tunnel under the snow, looking for worms, insects, and plant roots-anything they can eat. Squirrels leave their leafy tree nests to eat twigs, buds, and bark. In wintertime snow covers the ground. They smell along the ground to find the nuts they buried in fall. Squirrels and birds are active in the short hours of daylight. Severe weather, involving heavy snow accumulation and ice storms, can cause stress on wildlife. Plants and animals have to be able to adapt to low temperatures and a shortage of food. Forest animals that have not stored food for winter must struggle through deep snow to find a meal. Deer eat buds and twigs on the low branches of trees and bushes. Foxes hunt for rabbits and mice. In winter, the forest glistens with loads of cottony white snow meticulously heaped on every silhouette of branches. Walking there makes you long for the warmth of the fireside, the company of friends, and the joyous return of spring and new life. Fall means pretty much one thing to most wildlife: winter is right around the corner. They're scrambling to make sure they have everything they need to survive the cold.

Birds are lucky in being able to fly. Some species fly off to a warmer climate. Wild fruits and seeds are an important source of food for all birds that stay during the winter. They fluff out their feathers on cold days to help keep themselves warm.

'cold-blooded' vertebrates hide away in the winter under stones and logs-all sorts of places where they may be safe from hungry predators. Many invertebrates hide themselves away too. There is no doubt that winter is a difficult time if you are an invertebrate. Some species of invertebrates overwinter as adults under a log, stone or in a hole, and stay there throughout the cold months. Autumn is a time of preparation for mammals. Mammals that find it most difficult to cope in winter are those which rely mainly on invertebrates for their food. Most invertebrates are hard to find during the winter. Insectivorous mammals survive by slowing their body processes to almost a standstill -and they do this by hibernating. Certain mammals have what many people might consider the good fortune to be able to sleep through the winter—to hibernate. They bed down in the fall and, for all intents and purposes, don't arise again until spring. Some sleep very deeply while others slumber more lightly. Sleeping, snug in the snow, some animals hibernate to escape the cold. They also do this because it is really hard to find food during the winter. Winter is the most stressful time of the year for most forms of life. Mid-winter is very quiet in nature. And so gray that it's hard to tell where the ground ends and the sky starts. Snowflakes fall silently. Wind sighs in the branches of trees making cracking noises. A deep tranquility descends upon the forest in December.

All remnants of summer have vanished, each day is shorter than the last, and hopes for spring lie imprisoned in the tiny, dormant buds on deciduous trees and shrubs. The pale sun, ever low in the southern sky, visit's the winter woods briefly, if at all. However, don't let a decrease in activity appear as if there is nothing going on in the woods. Nature is not dead-it only rests and tolerates at the same time. Now that the leaves are off the trees and on the ground, we tend to feel that nature's processes have stopped for winter. However, this is when the recycling of leaves is just beginning. At first, the leaves, still bright with color, blanket the ground with a multicolored quilt that is equally as spectacular as when those same leaves were still at the tops of trees. But that loose, fluffy layer doesn't last long. Rain pounds the now-brown blades and presses them down against the soil. Snow compacts the blanket of fallen leaves. Now that the leaf litter is flattened on the forest floor, a new, and reverse, process begins. Soil that nourished new growth is waterlogged. Seeds are living organisms and respire just like other living organisms. They uptake oxygen and release carbon dioxide as a waste product. Seeds sown in very wet soil will not be able to exchange gases with the atmosphere and will, consequently, suffocate and die. Winter may cause the heart to sink, but, the memories of garden friends will lift the spirit. Thoughts of springtime restore the mind. The radiant sun yields to a softly lit moon. Dormancy takes back the flowers.

But, not everything sleeps. Beneath the top layer of soil, new life passes time in the darkness. Decay bacteria and fungi release nutrients from the spent bodies of dead organisms. Probably the most important are the bacteria. They are one-celled microscopic life forms. They are not animals, but a group of living things all their own. Soil bacteria feed on the complex sugars and other parts of leaves. The root-like strands of fungi are doing the same thing as they grow into the once- living tissue. Little by little, all the complex parts of the once-green leaves are taken apart. New seedlings will remove the available organic matter and the existing inorganic mineral material from the soil as the plant grows. Almost everything the plant takes in will have been recycled by the tireless toil of small decomposers that break down the lifeless bodies of dead organisms and the waste products in the soil breaking the energy bond built by photosynthesis, and converting complex sugars back to simple carbon dioxide and water. Decaying organic matter makes the soil thick and rich. Rock is the source of all soil mineral materials and the origin of all plant nutrients with the exceptions of nitrogen, hydrogen and carbon. The nature of soil is determined by what sort of parent rock it develops from, because this is its prime material. Together with all the living soil organisms it sustains soil acts as a sort of bank into which deposits and withdrawals are constantly made. A steady deposit of mineral material and organic matter keeps the soil alive.

The soil may appear to be without life, but unseen processes occur below the surface of the soil. The chilled soil only marks time. Humus is composed of partly decomposed plant and animal remains. When plants drop leaves, twigs, and other material to the ground, it piles up. This material is called leaf litter. Fallen leaves act as a wildlife boon enriching soil and providing a down-like comforter for soil organisms. When animals die, their remains add to the litter. Over time, all this litter decomposes, that is it decays, or breaks down, into its most basic chemical elements. As humus decomposes, its components are changed into forms usable by plants. Mineralogically, the smallest particles are clays which form a sticky mass when wet and hard clods when dry. Silt particles are intermediate in size and have a powdery, silky texture when dry. The largest particles are sands which do not stick together and feel gritty when rubbed between the fingers. Earthworms aerate the soil and help mix humus with minerals in the soil. Eventually all humus becomes completely decomposed, but in nature it is always being replaced as plants and animals die and give up their parts. Therefore it never really breaks down completely. Death becomes a way of restoring life. Concealed in the fertile soil, tiny organisms thrive in a subterranean realm. A teaspoon of good soil should contain literally billions of beneficial bacteria, thousands of protozoan, and miles of mycorrhizal fungi.

These organisms and larger life such as earthworms create a soil food web, consuming small bits of organic matter in the soil, converting it into nutrients. Plant roots can then take in those nutrients to produce leaves, stems, flowers, fruit, and seed. Leaf-litter decomposition is a vital process: this is how nutrients stored in leaves are recycled, returning to the soil and becoming available for the trees to take up again. Undisturbed within the soil, perennials wait for the return of the sun to free captive roots from icy confinement. The meadow grasses keep watch over the waiting fields for the return of warm season companions. The anticipated reunion shows the relationship between the productive soil and the plants growing in its nurturing medium. Plants fueled by the energy of the sun prepare for the copious alliance which they share with it. Wooded paths, lush foliage and blooms are only the beginning. A bright new world will shine with brilliant colors. Blooming crocuses, daffodils, and tulips will spice the morning air. Before spring comes, the trees are dark, the grass is brown and the ground is covered in snow. But if you wait, leaves unfurl and flowers blossom, the grass turns green and the mounds of snow melt down. Groggy animals awaken from slumber to view sights outside their winter shelter. Attentive ears hear sounds unheard since winter laid down its frozen veil. Spring brings with it new life offering new vegetation, animals, and protection. It also provides new homes and food as well.

As the weather warms and new growth emerges, the air fills with sounds almost forgotten. Birds returning to the forest, fields, and wetlands will find much needed rest in their spring refuge. The return of migrating songbirds in spring after an exhausting flight confirms that the end of winter has come. Cheerful singers whose quick calls trip up and down the scales, giving life to the dusky evening will arrive after traveling across half a continent—to return home. Buntings will begin returning from Central America to the U.S. to nest. Although we think of January and February as a slow deliberate journey through winter, it truly is a steady climb toward the warmth of spring. Trees sprout fresh new growth embellishing their sturdy frames. Understory shrubs growing beneath them produce leaves, flowers, and later fruit ushering in a new division of the year. A variety of birds, including vireos, and some warblers will use the shrub layer for foraging and nesting. Bluebirds, robins, cardinals, and finches will sing to find a mate. The best is yet to come, but first winter must be endured. The soil keeps secret that which has already come and that which is yet to come. While the outer leaves and above-ground foliage may die back, life lies in wait in the roots and core of perennial plants. Annual plants die in the fall after they scatter their seeds directly on the ground or include them in fruit that is consumed by animals and deposited elsewhere. Last year's bits and pieces linger above the ice-covered surface of the soil.

Warm rain turns to freezing snow as the weather steadily gets colder. Flowers that adorned the scenery have been reduced to memory. Annuals have disappeared. Only dried up stems remain as markers over their soil grave. Change was their Cain. Making seeds for reproduction is the culmination of the lifecycle of flowering plants. After that, a gradual decline begins. Two options are subsequently available. Either growth slows until a resting stage is reached, or growth slows until cessation. Some plants grow, produce flowers, set seeds, and retreat back into the soil to pass the winter as root stock. Other plants grow, produce flowers, set seeds, and die-all in one year. Nothing brightens up a garden like long blooming annuals, but many people don't want to replant every year. Luckily, if left to produce seeds, many annuals reseed themselves. For some the death-bell has rung. Death's dark angel has come to escort them to the banks of the Stygian shore. For others, their rest is temporary. Annuals sprout from seed, flower, set seed, and die within a single season. Most annuals are planted in spring and are killed by frost in the fall. But while they adorn our world, no other group of flowering plants provides so much color as quickly. Unlike annuals which need to replenish every year, perennial plants continue to beautify the landscape and give years of visual enjoyment. Perennial plants grow and bloom during the warm part of the year, with the foliage dying back in winter. Perennial plants come in two types.

They have either soft, non-woody stems that die back to the ground each winter, or they have hardened, woody stems that must withstand exposure to cold winter temperatures. Perennial plants are usually better competitors than annual plants, dominating most natural ecosystems. This is due to larger root systems which can access water and nutrients deeper in the soil and to earlier emergence in the spring. Perennials are a great choice for people who don't have a burning desire to dig in the dirt. You plant them once, and you're done. During the growing season all energy is put into growing and producing flowers. During the long lull all energy is put into maintaining basic metabolic processes. Survival at this uncertain time depends on how successful a plant or an animal is at adapting to the rise and fall of the mercury. The unrelenting war waged by insects on plants has come to an end. An insect with an empty stomach will survive lower subfreezing temperatures more so than an insect with a full stomach. This is because food in the stomach attracts water that can freeze and promote the growth of ice crystals. Insects don't have the benefit of body fat, like mammals do, to survive freezing temperatures and keep internal fluids from turning to ice. Many insects prepare for the cold by making their own antifreeze. During the fall, insects produce glycerol, which gives the insect body "supercooling" ability, allowing body fluids to drop below freezing points without causing ice damage.

In spring, glycerol levels drop again. Many insects don't survive the freezing cold temperatures but some do survive and they will pass on their vigor to future generations. There are three strategies for surviving inclement weather conditions; migration, dormancy, and toughing it out. Many species migrate between seasons. Many birds migrate in the fall. Many species undergo metabolic changes that allow them to "sleep" through winter. This is a very special, very deep sleep. Many species have adapted to being active during the winter. They must adapt to changes. Trees are bare and lawns are brown. Woodlands and marshes teaming with wildlife only a few months ago are comparatively still. Don't be fooled by appearance alone. Beneath winter's icy cover, many animals have adapted to seasonal changes in temperature and light in a way that is rather remarkable. A walk in the woods often reveals that there is more going on than meets the eye and that you are never truly alone. Animal tracks imprinted in the snow prove that even throughout the winter, activity and movement abounds. What could be more mysterious than the tell-tale signs of an unseen presence? Finding animal tracks offers a glimpse into a world that we might not otherwise see. Looking over these fragile signs makes you wonder what animal was here and what was it doing? Tracks and slides along streams indicate mink are close by in the cattail marshes and in swamps where they forage for crayfish, frogs, fishes, small mammals, and invertebrates.

Like their cousins the otters, mink will slide down snowy inclines on their belly. Only winter's severity remains as a final obstacle. A dark shroud has descended upon the land. The warmth of spring is a memory. Each year as the snow begins to accumulate, many of us assume that the animals have bedded down for the winter, sleeping away the cold winter days and nights, awaiting the spring thaw. For a few small mammals, winter survival depends on the snow itself, and the deeper the better. In the subnivean zone life goes on even as the surface world is locked up in icy confinement. In reality, the snow actually creates a unique sheltered environment for some small animals, allowing them to stay fairly active during the winter months. This band of lifesaving warmth supports a secret society of small mammals tunneling, making dens, eating food stashes-and one another- all winter long. To find a red squirrel in winter, look under the snow, not up in a tree. They dig cozy dens in the subnivean zone, burrowing tunnels down through the snow to stashes of coniferous cones that they cut and bury throughout the late summer and fall. Tiny two ounce voles are among the subnivean zone's most populous residents and are prolific tunnel builders. Unfortunately for voles, they are a primary food source for larger carnivores, and only about 10 percent of voles survive winter.

Weasels, called ermine when they turn white in winter, sport sleek bodies that allow them to snake through snow tunnels dug by their favorite winter prey-mice, voles, and red squirrels. Larger carnivores, like coyotes and foxes, listen for small mammals rustling around beneath the snow and then pounce, crashing through the quiet, protective realm of the subnivean zone. Tiny tracks in the snow disappear into a small hole in the snow. The tiniest twitch in the tall grass causes a reaction from a lone sentry perched within the broad crown of an oak tree. A second movement is detected in the tangled thatch and moist grass intensifying the focus from above. When a field mouse emerges through the accumulation of soft white snow from deep in the subnivean layer, the eyes in the sky prompt a silent but soon to become deadly descending flight in a precise arc toward the unsuspecting target. Within seconds, life at the lower level of the food chain ends for the mouse as its body is enclosed in the death grip of the powerful talons of one of the most efficient hunters. There are four stout, sharp talons on each of the red-tail's feet. Birds of prey have three talons in front and one behind. They are needle-sharp. The red-tailed hawk has been master of such aerial attacks for eons. Observing this large and powerful bird is akin to a spiritual experience.

The red-tailed hawk has made a spectacular come back since it was at risk by the same poisonous pesticides that once threatened the bald eagle, the symbol of our country, and by cash bounties intended to prevent large birds of prey from preying on farm animals. Red-tailed hawks seem comfortable in a variety of habitats, but prefer to nest at the edge of woods for easy access to open grasslands and for a panoramic view of their spacious surroundings. Although some red-tails will migrate, most hawks are permanent year round residents commonly seen in the mini-habitat along our highways. The snow covered fields can impede small rodent hunting, but birds and rabbits that venture out on a warm winter day often never live to regret being spotted by scanning eyes. It would be a sad day if we no longer saw the great redtail sailing over the tree tops on its broad expanse of wing and ruddy tail, or soaring upward in majestic circles until lost to sight in the ethereal blue, or a mere speck against the clouds. The length of daylight increases, the ice melts, and roots desperate for a drink take in water.

The landscape comes alive as an array of living things return to grace their world and ours. As we look forward to the daffodils pushing up out of the ground, don't wish winter away, but enjoy today and make the most of it. Snow covers up cold ground containing the odds and ends of last season.

Leaves, packed together between the dormant grass and an icy veneer, are a crucial pathway for nutrient return to the soil. Snow dusted trees are clad in white. Shadows of deciduous trees stand in solitude. Wooden frames don the ivory shawl. An outer covering of bark allows them to harbor the grudge. It's time to settle old scores and grapple with the indomitable forces of nature. Trees can withstand winter's assault. But their soft-stemmed allies must retreat into the dark abyss. During the summertime, when the deciduous trees still have all their leaves, evergreens are often a forgotten component of the landscape. They keep a low profile, while their deciduous counterparts have their summer fling and take all the glory. But just as the tortoise in the Aesop's fable, the motto of the evergreens is "slow and steady wins the race". As the year wears on and the foliage of the flowering shrubs retreats, evergreens reemerge in the landscape. In the absence of any competition, they can now grab the spotlight. Winter sun, wind, and cold temperatures can bleach and desiccate evergreen foliage, damage bark, and injure or kill branches, flower buds, and roots. Snow and ice can break branches and topple entire trees. Winter food shortages force mice, rabbits and deer to feed on bark, twigs, flower buds, and foliage, injuring and sometimes killing trees and shrubs.

Even though plants respond differently to winter stress and each winter provides a different set of stressful conditions, plants possess a remarkable ability to withstand extremely

Shadows of deciduous trees stand in solitude.

severe winter conditions. Evergreens have needle-like foliage that remains green throughout the winter. Perennials root stock is hardy enough to survive a cold winter. Bulbs can survive the winter in warmer climates but must be dug up in colder climates. Most people don't think about trees having to survive the winter. That's probably because we see the same trees year after year and they tend to look pretty much the same. Just as their furred, finned, and feathered brothers and sisters, trees have been "tested" by evolutionary fires-their adaptations are pure and proven genius. A tree is interesting, complex and busy all year long. Always changing, adapting, growing, preparing, re-growing, it knows what to do, how to survive. Incredibly, some of its details are still a mystery to science. They are rather inspiring. A tree's needs depend on weather, not the calendar. Conditions such as air temperature, rainfall and soil temperature will affect how soon a tree loses its leaves, stops growing and enters dormancy. While fall color seems to get all the attention, it's what trees do later in autumn that is the most stunning, if harder to see. Some of these later changes seem to border on magic. Leafless tree branches set against a snowy backdrop create a rather bleak scene.

And while it might appear lifeless, deciduous trees have several strategies to survive the cold and dark conditions of winter. Winter is a challenging time for all living things, including trees. Cold harms plant tissue by turning water to ice within the cells, forming crystals that can damage them. Trees have evolved to survive winter by going dormant. That means not just dropping leaves and slowing or stopping growth, but also reducing the amount of water in branch and root tissue. The lowered concentration of water in a tree's tissue acts like a natural antifreeze: it means it takes deeper cold to form ice inside them. Liquid water in the winter can be found underground and in the snow. The water in the soil around the roots may freeze solid, but the cold won't hurt the roots themselves until water inside their tissues start to freeze. Even though snow will keep roots insulated, it can be a heavy burden on the branches. Snow and ice can sometimes get too heavy for branches to support, causing them to bend and snap. Loss of too much water, without replacement, will kill cells. This can happen in winter, especially among conifers. If roots cannot replace liquid water lost through needles, then tissue dies. Evergreen groves provide a sheltered place to settle in for the long nights during the cold months for great horned owls. The nighttime belongs to these big, bulky owls, the largest of American "eared" owls.

With a wing span of over four feet, their massive size and potent strength allow great horned owls to occupy the upper portion of the food pyramid as top predator in the woods. Look at the treeline silhouetted against the winter-white sky, and you might see a napping owl. A keen sense of sight and an acute sense of hearing aid extremely sharp talons. Visually stunning, the great horned owl spends the majority of its time hunting. Owls are stealth hunters. Fluffy feathers give them almost silent flight. From a quiet perch, the owl listens for sounds that betray an animal's presence. They may move from tree to tree to get a better fix on the source of the sound. Once they pinpoint the sound, the owl silently swoops in, spreads its talons wide and pounces on its prey -known as the "perch and pounce" hunting method. Hardy enough to withstand cold winter weather, the big owl is one of the first birds to nest, laying its pure white eggs when there is still snow on the ground beneath its annexed nest of twigs. Typically the female lays two eggs, sometimes more when food is abundant. They may start laying their eggs as early as late January. There are reasons why nesting activities are begun so early. It takes owls a long time to grow up. Because it is so cold at the time of nesting, incubation begins immediately after each egg is laid. As a consequence, the eggs hatch in sequence, which gives the first hatchling a size advantage over its siblings.

If food is scarce, the largest will out- compete the others for food that the parents bring back to the nest and only one may survive. There are two reasons owls rule our winter skies. Owls keep warm with the help of down feathers close to their bodies. But, they have another trick up their wings! Owls also have specialized contour feathers with extra extensions that serve to trap even more heat next to their bodies. Owls, like all of the other forest creatures that have learned to defy winter, know how to play the survivor game. Although the initial assault was short-lived, the soil remains cold. For now, a truce has been declared. The white flag has been raised. The cease fire is temporary. The struggle to stay alive during winter will continue until spring arrives in victory. Loss of life may be high depending on the duration and severity of winter. Those that survive will be made stronger. They will pass on that vigor. The weak will perish with the melting snow. The transition from winter to spring represents the triumph of life over death. The wintry Legion marches on. Those that survive winter will feel the warmth of spring. Seeing pretty, snow-covered landscapes and being bundled up in a blanket sipping hot coca is nice for a little while but the cold weather has overstayed its welcome. Though you can't do anything to speed up the arrival of spring, you can start thinking more positively! There is something about late February and early March that brings about stints of somber moods.

A fail-safe tonic to cure the late winter blues is to take a walk in the woods. Ah, March. It's the time of the year when the weather can trick you into thinking it's spring one day, only to smack you in the face with sleet and snow the next. When the last late winter storm has passed, the white of the clouds, the blue of the sky, and the red of the sunset will signal the end of another season. Each winter, spring seems a little slower to arrive than in past years. Perhaps the reason is an increased longing for the long-awaited signs of spring as we get older. Spring is a time of renewal and rebirth. It's that exciting time of the year when you can almost watch nature burst with everything new. A flower that's still a bud in the morning will be wide open by lunchtime. There's something new growing around every corner every day. Now is the time to go and enjoy all the beauty as long as it is in that wonderful condition of freshness. It only lasts shortly though, a few weeks and the exciting fireworks are over. The world seems filled with new life and new hope. It is a time of change. Finally! From the dreary, deadened shadows of winter's gloom sprouts spring. Lady Spring arrives in the magical world of woodland wonderland dressed in her gossamer gowns of tender new leaves and blossoms. There are flowering trees and new leaves everywhere when spring begins to peek its lovely head around the corner. The warmth of the sun awakens something within us. You can drink it in like the elixir of life. A perennial plant's life cycle revolves around the seasons.

When winter comes, the plant enters a period of dormancy. It sheds its leaves and retreats into a kind of hibernation to protect itself against the cold. This season of inactivity is key to the plant's revival in spring. Tiny snowdrops appear from nowhere under the trees as a prelude to the awakening of Nature into a new life of warmth, sunshine, abundance and color. The crocuses are getting ready to announce themselves; and the trees are whispering new life. Spring bulbs such as daffodils, hyacinths and early tulips will likely grow up through the snow and cold with no adverse effects, other than possibly some browning of the leaves and flower tips. The same will be true for perennial flowers and early spring shrubs that will leaf out and bloom. They can deal with sub-freezing temperatures and will be fine. Once clandestine signs of spring defy the last attempts of winter to hang on. The trees and shrubs tolerate frigid cold and dustings of snow, but if you listen closely, you can almost hear them snoring. This is the time when we have to practice trust-we've watched our perennials go through a process that looks exactly like death, and we've watched every leaf fall off the trees, and on especially cold days even the most beautiful scenery looks a little bleak. The sky is deceitfully blue. The sun shines, but offers little heat. The moon reflects the sun's light, but declines to illuminate the darkness. Plants need food, water, and sunshine. Animals need food and water, and most of them love sunlight, but there are some that hide from it.

Many animals get their food from plants, but some feed on other animals that they kill. Everything alive has its time to rest and sleep. Most plants and some animals sleep a part of each year. The time they take to sleep depends on the climate where they live. In cold climates plants sleep in the winter. We know they are going to sleep when their leaves begin to fall. When the cold winter comes they stand so bare that they look as though they are dead. When the trees begin to feel the warmer days of spring the sap starts to flow again from their roots. It goes up the trunk of the tree and into each branch. The waiting buds begin to swell. Before we know it the trees are again dressed in green. Many plants do not live through the winter. Instead, each spring a new plant grows from a little seed. The tiny seed grows and develops into a plant that eventually blossoms. When fall drives away summer, the seeds become ripe and the first frost kills the mother plant. There are many animals that go to sleep when fall comes. They remain asleep until spring wakes them up. The first warm day brings them out of their winter home. The warmth causes plants to grow and food becomes more abundant. Forest wildflowers push shoots above ground in spring, taking advantage of the sunlight they receive before trees grow leaves and shade them. The earth and air are full of life, where just a short time before everything seemed dead. As the temperature outside begins to drop, noticeable changes take place all around us.

Squirrels get busy gathering nuts, leaves change colors and begin to drop, and the birds start their journey south. As winter gets closer, we start seeing fewer and fewer animals. Animals are not the only living things preparing for winter each year. Plants, unlike animals can't take up their roots and move off to a more protected place when unfavorable weather happens. They just have to sit and bear it. Both plants and animals are programmed to face cold weather in several different ways. All living things must adapt to their environment in order to survive. As the mercury plunges and days get shorter, plants and animals switch to winter mode. When winter sets in, trees stop growing and go dormant to save energy. Soon winter is here. Snow covers the ground. And the effects of winter linger on and on. The quiet woods may seem lifeless in winter, but it's not. Most of the snow and ice are gone. In the dark corners of the woods, winter is becoming spring. Day after day the weather is getting warmer and the sun shines more brightly. After winter has slipped by, we'll be well into spring, the trees will start to green up and all the usual spring flowers will come in all colors, sizes, and blooms. But not yet! In this in between time we must wait a little longer, we must hope and believe.

A walk through the winter woods offers adventures that a summertime hike could never provide. But getting past the silence and empty branches requires a different pace and a new way of seeing. If you see small holes dug in the snow,there's a good chance a squirrel made it while searching for a nut hidden last fall.The acorns they don't find might become oak seedlings in the spring. After a fresh snowfall, it's amazing to see the activity in forests and fields as animals come out of their sheltering places to find food. Woodpeckers make surprisingly large holes in trees in their determined quest to get at the insects living under the bark. Tiny holes show that insects are at work under the bark,which can sometimes lead to the demise of the tree. A snowy stroll reveals some suspicious characters traveling on foot, and a secret world beneath them. Tracks in the snow have a lot more to tell than merely who walked by. The tiny prints of a deer mouse disappear in the snow. Then the telltale brushstrokes of owl wings, framing its last step come into view,a reminder that in spite of how much goes on at the surface, an equally busy world plays out beneath the snow.